KNITTING RULES!

STEPHANIE PEARL-McPHEE

Storey Publishing

*The mission of Storey Publishing is to serve our customers
by publishing practical information that encourages personal
independence in harmony with the environment.*

Edited by Deborah Balmuth
Art direction and text design by Mary Velgos
Cover design by Mary Velgos and Kimberly Glyder
Text production by Mary Velgos and Jennifer Jepson Smith
Cover photographs by Adam Mastoon
Illustrations by © Diana Marye Huff
Illustration coordination by Ilona Sherratt
Indexed by Diane Brenner

The information in this book is true and complete to the best of our knowledge. All recommendations
are made without guarantee on the part of the author or Storey Publishing. The author and publisher
disclaim any liability in connection with the use of this information. For additional information please
contact Storey Publishing, 210 MASS MoCA Way, North Adams, MA 01247.

Storey books are available for special premium and promotional uses and for customized editions.
For further information, please call 1-800-793-9396.

Printed in the United States by Versa Press
10 9 8 7 6 5 4 3 2

Library of Congress Cataloging-in-Publication Data

Pearl-McPhee, Stephanie.
    Knitting rules! / Stephanie Pearl-McPhee.
       p. cm.
    Includes index.
    ISBN-10: 1-58017-834-0; ISBN-13: 978-1-58017-834-1 (pbk. : alk. paper)
    1. Knitting. I. Title.
TT820.P3745 2006
746.43'2—dc22
                                                        2006004622

For Janine

*whose constant ability to find bright joy
in the mundane is deeply missed.*

With thanks to:

My mate, Joe, for putting up with . . . well. He knows what he puts up with.

My beautiful and clever daughters, Amanda, Megan, and Samantha, for not turning into delinquents while I wrote this book.

My mum, Bonnie, for not letting me turn into a delinquent while I wrote this book.

My siblings, Ian, Ali, and Erin . . . for making out like all the knitting is cool.

My nephew, Hank, for being five years old and wanting to learn how to knit. (I forgive you for breaking the ball winder.)

My long suffering friends, Lene, Ken, Cassandra, Emma, and Denny. I owe them all hand-knit socks.

My friend and agent, Linda Roghaar, for always picking up the phone and not sighing (too loudly) when I tell her my troubles.

Deborah Balmuth, crack editor; Pam Art, visionary; and everyone else at Storey Publishing who totally understands that no matter what the rest of the world thinks, you really can have a knitting-book emergency.

Finally, special thanks to every knitter I ever met, e-mailed, or ran into in a yarn shop. I'd know nothing without them.

CONTENTS

one

What is **KNITTING** and How Does it Get Like This?

IF YOU PICKED UP THIS BOOK, I probably don't need to convince you that knitting is great. It's more than possible, however, that you could use a little help explaining to people why you do it, or why you do it so much, or why you can't stop doing it.

The bare bones of knitting sound simple, and they are; sadly, this is probably the beginning of the confusion between those regular people known as *non-knitters,* and the enlightened, the extraordinary people we call *knitters.*

Non-knitters can't quite get it. You explain the basics of knitting to them, then tell them that you spend all of your money and all of your spare time on this pursuit, and inform them that you bitterly resent any time taken from it by ordinary activities like laundry and employment, and they'll look at you as if there's crazy all over you, like plaid on a Scotsman. You can show them all of your yarn (although I don't recommend this; revealing the size of the stash while you're trying to convince someone you're not nuts is counterproductive). You can even make them touch and hold it, and they're still going to wonder if you're a few sheep short of a flock.

Admittedly, if you think about it from the non-knitter's point of view, the statement "I play with string for several hours a day and never tire of it" does sound as if you're touched, but that's because the bare bones of knitting is not all there is. These non-knitters haven't lived the considerable charms of knitting or, even better than that, gotten themselves a Knitting Lifestyle.

Here's the whole idea of knitting. One stick holds loops of yarn and a second stick pulls a continuous piece of string through the loops, one by one. Row upon row is accomplished until you have a piece of knitted fabric.

THE SUBTLE PLEASURES OF KNITTING

Non-knitters don't understand that it all starts with the simplicity of pulling one loop through another (and that at first it ain't so simple). They don't understand that there's the detail of getting the loop to sit on the needle just right, or that you can knit two together, or wrap the yarn and get one more, or, horror of horrors, drop one and sit stunned, afraid that if you so much as breathe the stitch will run all the way down to the start and you'll never, ever get it picked up again. They don't know that all of this holds the key to a tiny little world of genius intrigue.

Non-knitters don't know what we do, that when we first learn to knit, this sort of thing is exceedingly high drama, that the thrill of getting it right is like skydiving (except, you know, safer), and that the defeat of messing up is as nasty as losing the Boston Marathon by 10 seconds to a guy who didn't even train. How about trying to tell them about the surprise of discovering that you aren't knitting what you thought you were? That due to some bizarre and repeated error on your part, you're making a tube top instead of socks and despite the really big difference between those two items, you cannot, for the life of you, explain why. They don't understand that knitting is surprising, perplexing, and gripping, as you loop stitch after stitch through each other and make Something.

If you find a non-knitter who thinks what you do is clever, beautiful, and artistic; who never asks for knitted stuff but wears it with pride when you give it to him or her; and will help you carry home a whole fleece or a stack of stitch dictionaries without once implying that you might want to get a grip — marry that person.

Knitting Rules!

Pointing out to non-knitters that as far as dorky habits go, running marathons and keeping a stamp collection are at least as pointless as knitting and don't even keep you warm in winter won't endear you to them. Furthermore, it doesn't make them think your knitting habit makes any more sense. Stick to your knitting and say nothing about rock collections or racing plastic boats. (You can think it, though. I would.)

ENDLESS CREATIVE POSSIBILITIES

Once you get the hang of the act of knitting, you get to discover its variations — knitting, purling, decreasing, increasing, cabling, yarn overs, intarsia, Fair Isle, entrelac, Estonian, Latvian . . . How about twined knitting or . . . my, the mind reels, and it's only the beginning. Do you do it left-handed or right? Pick or throw? Use stranding or bobbins? Wool or cotton? Circulars or straights? Use four or five double-pointed needles, or never touch them?

The techniques available to you can take a lifetime to learn and the different ways to make these loops with sticks is engaging, clever, and not at all monotonous. Non-knitters don't understand that there's always something left to learn, and trying to tell them that there are so many extremely interesting ways to do something with string is folly. They weren't interested in the first way to do it, never mind all the ways you've read about. Non-knitters usually stop you at this point and tell you that you're out of your tree. Ignore them. Knitters have it figured out. It is non-knitters (even though they out-number us) who haven't grasped the magic.

THE SPICE OF LIFE

I used to show yarn to non-knitters to help them understand. The materials we knit with are temptation itself. There's cotton, silk, and wool, for example, and fiber has come a long way in terms of sophistication. There's organic hand-dyed cotton, Italian crepe cotton, and Egyptian cotton spun fine for tiny lace caps. The silk could be softly spun, rustic, and slubby, or a floss that's almost as fine as the silkworm spun it and painted in colors that can break your heart.

That longtime standby, our fine friend wool, is no longer a sad itchy wallflower at the fiber ball; she has come into her glory. You can find hand-spun wool that's reminiscent of the sheep it left, cushy and bouncy, waiting to be warm mittens or a hat. There's thick bulky wool for cardigans as warm as coats, and merino spun so fine for lace knitting that the name *cobweb* is really appropriate. Hand-painted, soft spun, cabled, bouclé, self-patterning for socks. The list goes on and on, and we haven't even touched the world of man-made fibers. Railroad yarn that looks like it sounds, eyelash yarns that flutter fetchingly, hard-wearing acrylics so durable that you could use them to knit tires for trucks. I swear, no matter how your tastes run, your hour is now.

Turn me loose in a yarn shop and I can be at the cash register in four minutes with Shetland for the most traditional of sweaters or sequined rayon fun fur for a thong that a Vegas showgirl would think was over the top. It's enough to make knitters want to take off their clothes and roll around in their stash, but you can't tell that to non-knitters either. (Trust me. They don't understand

> **If you never leave the house without your knitting, and only a house fire would make you think twice, your knitting "hobby" may have become a lifestyle.**

the urge . . . not even if you show them cashmere.)

As stunning as it may seem to us, the non-knitters are immune. Completely immune. They can't understand where we get the time; they can't understand the compelling and fascinating difference between a 50/50 merino/silk blend and a 10/90 merino/silk blend. They can't understand yarn as souvenir, yarn as comfort, or knitting as intriguing. They think of knitting as both too simple and too complex. They believe they don't have time and that we're wasting our time — that knitting is both so boring they couldn't be bothered and too complex and difficult for them (but they still want the hand-knit socks).

Knitting and yarn appeal to the senses. A project in the works smells good, feels good, looks good. Never feel bad about wanting it hanging around. Knitting is too beautiful to be clutter. A half-finished shawl left on the coffee table isn't a mess: It's an objet d'art.

What non-knitters are missing is the personality-enhancing qualities of knitting. Knitting is a miracle worker. With knitting, people can suddenly do things they couldn't do before. They can wait in line without becoming impatient. They can sit through a grade-school concert with a smile. They can handle long meetings and lectures, all without bothering other people or pacing around like lunatics. I can think of several times in my own life when knitting kept me from slapping some fool upside the head.

Knitting makes boring people interesting and mundane things intriguing. The only other thing that does that has the disadvantage of giving you a hangover instead of a pair of socks.

It's okay to be confused when somebody tells you she could never knit because it looks too complicated and (in the same breath) that it's too boring to be able to stick to it. What she means is that she doesn't want to take up knitting.

AN EXAMINATION OF THE NON-KNITTER

Non-knitters are, to me, very interesting. . . . As knitters, it's good that we spend some time getting to understand their confusing ways.

According to my calculations, knitters (past and present) make up about 15 percent of the North American population. That's astounding when you think about it. It's enough for a revolution (imagine a world run by knitters?) or a cult. Cults and revolutions often end badly, however, so no matter what you're thinking, we should probably put it out of our heads. We are still fiercely outnumbered. Considering these odds, it's also pretty likely that you are going to have to marry/live with/date a non-knitter.

There are roughly 50 million knitters in North America. I suspect that knitting is a little bit like religion; many are not currently "practicing." This would explain why you can always find yourself the only knitter at a cocktail party.

FIVE REASONS WHY PEOPLE DON'T KNIT

Given the multitude of charms that knitting possess, why doesn't everyone knit? How come the other 85 percent of the world keeps looking at us like . . . that? A brief and unscientific study (I asked some people) revealed the reasons people say they don't knit.

Reason 1

"I could never do that. I'm completely uncoordinated." Right. Well, that's an interesting one. Considering that since we've invented knitting (sometime in the 14th century) it's been child labor in many parts of the world, I've got to tell you that this one doesn't hold water. I find it difficult to believe that children all over the world can manage to learn this, no matter how poorly educated or unskilled they are, but a full-grown person who can read, write, drive a car, and work the DVD player is unable to.

Reason 2 **"I could never do that; I don't have the patience."** I have the attention span of a three-year-old full of chocolate bars at a birthday party, so I'm not buying this one either. Knitting grants patience to those who do it. Ask around. Most knitters will tell you they're at their most patient with the needles in their hands, and that this practice makes them more tolerant of ordinary setbacks.

Reason 3 **"I can't afford it."** Nope. Real knitters (the ones who've fallen down hard and don't want to get up) would knit grass with sticks if they ran out of money. There are lots of ways to get by on the cheap.

Reason 4 **"I'm not smart enough."** Knitting, all knitting — every single item — is made up of two stitches, knit and purl. If you're wearing clothes and you dressed yourself, you're smart enough to knit. If you're wearing matching clothes or a coordinating accessory, you're smart enough to knit well.

Reason 5 **"I don't have time."** Don't start with me. We all find the time for what we love to do. Just admit it: You want to cross-stitch instead.

There are many kinds of knitters, and not all of them seem crazy when you look at them. There are knitters who have made their hobby a lifestyle and those who have a moderate, reasonable knitting habit that they engage in "some" of the time. Both kinds of knitters appear to be happy and (somewhat) well adjusted. Knowing which camp you fall into can help determine whether you should start planning a yarn stash for your old age.

Knitting is endlessly interesting. Knitting lets you turn one thing into another, and better than that, a variety of "anothers." A ball of yarn could be anything at all: a hat, a book cover, a bag. For the love of wool, Debbie New knit a boat. (It's seaworthy, too.) That innocent-looking string could be anything, and it's all up to the knitter.

IS KNITTING ADDICTIVE?

Many of us have been trying to figure this out for years, but it's a difficult question. First, yarn and knitting seem to affect different people differently. It could be a matter of genetics, availability, or experience, but not all knitters will end up with behavior that indicates addiction. There do appear to be several levels of yarn, uh, "involvement."

Level 1 **Interested.** The knitter engages in yarn activities some of the time, mostly in social settings in yarn shops or at lessons, or quietly in his or her free time. This knitter may attend a knitting club or guild, and may sometimes purchase yarn, though it doesn't really affect the budget much. The "interested" knitter has firm, concrete plans for all of the yarn. She occasionally bypasses a yarn store for a bookstore.

Level 2 **Focused.** The knitter now often "knits alone" and frequently allows her family to see her knitting. The "focused" knitter may now be actively trying to recruit friends and family into her yarn lifestyle and has been seen purchasing yarn with no clear intentions, just because it is "soft" or "on sale." This knitter may have several projects on the needles, and may actually be overwhelmed (occasionally and happily) with her own knitty plans. She still goes to bookstores and imagines herself putting down the knitting to read. (She doesn't.)

Level 3 **Preoccupied.** The knitter may now be spending all of her free time knitting but is still attending to other things, like job and children. The "preoccupied" knitter actively shops for yarn often, discusses yarn often, and occasionally has dreams in which knitting figures prominently. In a bookstore, she now treks only to the knitting book section.

Level 4 **Obsessed.** The knitter spends all of her free time knitting, and the time she considers "free" is expanding. She is likely now neglecting housework with a vengeance and is dreaming in knitting code. The "obsessed" knitter stalks other people to stare at their sweaters, and would rather sit on a train for nine hours where she can knit comfortably, rather than drive. This knitter has discovered books on tape, buys yarn like it's a job, and dreams of a way to make money from knitting

We will never know whether knitters are addicted to yarn or to the act of knitting. To find out, we'd need to take someone's yarn away and see how she feels. I can't do that to another knitter. The ethical questions are too tricky.

so she wouldn't have to waste good knitting time earning a living. People in the neighborhood have started calling this person things like "that knitting guy" and the knitter does not care. Quite the contrary, he is flattered and has never been happier.

ASSESS YOUR LEVEL OF OBSESSION

Scenario 1 *You and a friend are in a restaurant and while you're waiting for the food, you're (naturally) knitting. The waitress comes to the table with your water and says, "Wow, is that knitting? I've always wanted to knit." You:*

A Take out the spare needles and yarn you have in your bag (for just this kind of moment) and, telling her that there was a time in your life when you too were a non-knitter, plop her down at your table and teach her how to knit in between courses.

B Ask her what she's always dreamed of knitting and encourage her to meet you at the stitch-and-bitch you attend downtown.

C Show her how stitches are formed on the needles, extol the joys of precision, and encourage her to get a book about the concepts of knitting.

D Give her some beautiful yarn and needles, as it will all come together when she's ready.

E Say, "That's nice. Is there any lemon for my water?"

Scenario 2 *When you wear your new shawl to a party, a woman comes up to you and compliments it. "That's so beautiful," she says. "Did you make that?" You reply:*

A "Yes, I did, and you can make one too!"

B "Yes, and I'm considering making one in blue. Would

you like to see the reverse side?"

(C) "Do you like it? I changed the gauge from 20 to 18 stitches to 4 inches and I think it really paid off.

(D) "Thank you, I'm glad it's the right size. The last one I knit blocked out so big that it ended up as big as a car cozy."

(E) "Thanks. I got it at Wal-mart."

Scenario 3 *There's a sale at your favorite neighborhood yarn shop.* You:

(A) Tell all your friends, knitting and non-knitting, then arrange a car pool and knitting lessons for afterward.

(B) Tell no one (you don't want the competition), but go quietly to the shop first thing in the morning and score that 850 yards of mohair you've been coveting.

(C) Go to the sale, but use your stash spreadsheet to make sure you're getting only the 500 pounds of yarn you really need.

(D) Go enthusiastically but buy very little, as the big box you bought at the last sale is still at the front door. Besides, you're really into spinning your own yarn right now.

(E) Go, buy lots of yarn, have a wonderful time, then put it in your closet.

Scenario 4 *Seduced by a good-looking sweater pattern and a yummy yarn, you've begun a new project that's not really working out (by "not working out," I mean the sweater resembles a sweater the way a nun resembles yak fur).* You:

(A) Take the sweater to your wide circle of knitting friends or have one of the more experienced club members help sort things out.

(B) Pour a glass of your choice of liquid concentration, then sit down with needles and yarn and experiment with the various decreases and stitch patterns you know until you've worked it out.

C Go online and check for correction to the pattern, then when you find none, pull out some graph paper and a pencil and work up a chart, using a calculator to rejig the stitch counts.

D Keep knitting, wondering what it's going to turn out to be.

E What sweater? You're at the local pub with the Thursday-night stitch-and-bitch group. Who has time to knit?

If your answers are mostly A, you are a Missionary. Missionary knitters are those knitters who, regardless of their skill level, are compelled to spread the word of the knit. Convinced (and quite rightly) that knitting is the best thing since sliced bread, they're forever attempting to spread the word of wool and convert ordinary people into knitters. Their enthusiasm is infectious and they're generous with lessons, time, and knitting supplies. Their motto is "Don't knock it till you try it" and they're the visionaries of the knitting world. Missionaries are by nature giving people, and will often make a gift of yarn and needles to a fledgling knitter to entice her and keep her knitting. Sometimes called "pushers" by other knitters, missionaries

> There are lots of kinds of knitters, and all forms get you into the club. You can be a card-carrying, die-hard knitter the first moment you knit the first row on your first fluffy scarf or you might not feel like a knitter until right after you finish an Aran sweater with a 48-inch chest and cables so complex that you had to get NASA to help you chart it.

will always encourage a stash-enhancing trip, never turn down a knitting social event, and are usually the head of the local knitting club.

If your answers are mostly B, you are a Sensei. Senseis have elevated knitting to a lifestyle. Never without needles and yarn, there's nothing knitting senseis don't know, and many of them are natural teachers. Through a combination of experience, education, and good instincts, knitting senseis are walking knitting textbooks. Wondering how to make the top of a sock stretchy enough? Knitting senseis know a dozen cast-ons. Mis-cross a cable 17 rows ago? Knitting senseis can show you how to fix the mistake without ripping back. Knitting senseis never wonder whether a knitting project would be too difficult for them. If they haven't done it, it's because they choose not to. Knitting senseis know all, see all, and fear nothing. If they weren't so damned helpful, you would hate them. You'll recognize a sensei by their confident knitting style, the stacks of complex patterns, and stashes that rival the gross national product of a small country.

If your answers are mostly C, you are a Scientist. Knitting scientists are identified by the stuff in their knitting bags: a calculator, graph paper, and a palm pilot with a spreadsheet detailing their stash. Never caught unready, knitting scientists swatch religiously, calculate gauge to the quarter stitch, and plot decreases according to a rate of slope that they have personalized for their own body type. Mortified to turn out a sweater with a wonky neckline, scientists place more focus on the technical aspect of knitting. They tend to be methodical stashers, usually buying yarn with a project in mind. This does nothing to limit the size of their stash, but does organize it somewhat. Knitting scientists are likely the only knitters who can put their hands on a tape measure in less than five minutes.

If your answers are mostly D, you are an Organic Knitter. Organic knitters are all about the process. Utterly relaxed about gauge and swatching, organics knit happily along, unconcerned and (mostly) uncaring about the outcome of a project. Organics are all about the yarn, the feel and the act of knitting, and embrace the full yarn family of activities. Occasionally organics are that rare breed of knitter known as the "multi-crafter," moving surely among weaving, crochet, and knitting and often combining several approaches. Organics can be identified with certainty when you overhear the phrase "No, I didn't swatch — it will fit somebody." Another characteristic is their longing to so fully embrace knitting that they have earnest discussions about about how to get a flock of sheep into an urban townhouse backyard.

If your answers are mostly E, you are a Pretender. These knitters are barely knitters, having been granted "knitter" status only by the virtue of their affection for the craft and the way they keep turning up. Pretenders buy lots of yarn and lots of patterns, show up at all the conferences and knitting meet-ups, but — inexplicably — don't seem to knit at all. Pretenders can be outed by careful observation. Have they been knitting the same blue garter-stitch scarf for six

Knitting Rules!

and a half years with no discernible progress? Pretenders (or knit supporters) are somehow immune to the charms of knitting, but have fallen head over heels for their community of knitters.

If you meet another knitter who's exactly your type, always try to get to the yarn shop ahead of her. She's your fiercest competition.

NO TIME TO KNIT?

There are more hours in a day for knitting than you think. The key to getting a lot of knitting done is multitasking.

TELEVISION WATCHING

This is prime knitting time. Most knitters get a lot done in front of the TV set. Within the genre, it is important to select programming to suit your knitting. Assess your project, then choose the appropriate show.

1 **Drama, romance, and the news.** Any of these is good for most any kind of knitting, as once you get a quick look, it's really all about the listening. Don't attempt projects that require counting during the news or weather reports, which often involve numbers that can confuse you.

2 **Action.** This requires actually seeing some of the show in order to follow the plot. Projects that allow you to look away without losing count or your place on a chart are the ticket here. Think plain socks, stockinette sweaters, garter stitch, and simple hats and mittens.

3 **Comedy.** This is a flexible genre. Humor that relies on the spoken word works as well as drama for any kind of knitting. Physical humor, however, is best for very simple knits, since knitting during this type of show means

you're either going to annoy the daylights out of the person you're watching with ("What happened?") or repeatedly rewind to see what you missed. Either way, you won't make good knitting time.

④ **Movies with subtitles.** This requires selecting a pattern that doesn't have a chart or complex stitch pattern, which are too tricky to read along with subtitles. Many knitters find this good motivation for learning a second language.

⑤ **Horror.** Knitting is probably the only thing that lets chickens like me watch a horror movie. I can gaze firmly at my knitting whenever a scene is too intense. Just be careful: a nasty fright can knock a goodly number of stitches off the needles.

MOVIES, THEATER, OR OPERA

Follow the same rules as for TV, but use extra caution and show extra consideration for those around you. Once you leave your home, rules of knitting politeness apply.

① **Use wooden or plastic needles.** The *click-click* of our needles can annoy the guy in front of us. If you use metal needles and the guy throws popcorn in your mohair, well, that's a reasonable response.

② **Knit something simple.** There's no way to turn on the lights if you make a mistake, waiting for a "daylight scene" is frustrating, and holding up your work to the screen to find your way will make your family refuse to go with you again. (P.S. A small flashlight annoys people too.)

③ **Unless there is carpet on the floor, use circulars over straights or DPNs.** I'm here to tell you that there's nothing like the unbelievably loud sound of a needle hitting the floor to make you want to eat your ball of sock yarn.

WORK TIME

Depending on your job there may be opportunities to combine earning a living with knitting. Can you get a headset so you can talk on the phone while you knit? Could you knit during meetings? (Remember to look up and make eye contact from time to time.) Can you pretend to be blind so someone will read your e-mail aloud to you?

TRANSPORTATION

A knitter is, by far and away, more willing than your average person to use a car pool or public transportation to get around. I turn out a pair of socks a month just using the subway instead of driving. Good for the environment, good for your knitting. Remember to choose a mate who likes to drive and you'll never mind getting in the car again.

EXERCISE

This is more difficult, but you can even combine knitting with a workout. Obviously, swimming and jogging are going to be tough, but a stationary bike is perfect. I could tell you a cautionary tale about avoiding knitting on a treadmill, but you might be smarter than I am. Many knitters have perfected walking and knitting: remember to wear something with pockets to hold your yarn and stick to small, lightweight projects. There are three things to remember when combining exercise with knitting:

1. Eyes front.
2. Yarn caught in machinery can have consequences more dire than tangled yarn.
3. Knitting, no matter how fast you do it, doesn't qualify as a cardio workout.

10 TIPS

Ten Tips for Identifying Your Own Kind

Not all knitters knit in public. I don't know why, but I think it might have something to do with the way people look at us. Considering how many kinds of knitters there are, it may be difficult to find each other in a crowd. These techniques can help.

1. Yell the word *mohair.* A knitter will look up from her activity.

2. In a loud voice, say, "Was that a moth?" A knitter will at the very least flinch, or, depending on the development of her stash, will leap up and run or faint.

3. Wear hand-knit stuff. It attracts knitters like bees to honey.

Knitting Rules!

4. Look for a woman with small round holes in her purse. These knitting needle puncture marks are a dead giveaway.

5. Knit in public. After 10 minutes, see who's watching you or inching her way closer.

6. In a large public space, loudly say, "I really don't know why anyone would buy cashmere yarn." See whose mouth opens.

7. At a party, lock yourself in a bathroom that has the kind of lock with the small round hole in the center. You'll be freed by the only person carrying a long thin stick. A knitter.

8. Leave out wool for bait. (Watch the trap. You don't want to lose the wool to a fast knitter.)

9. Randomly ask people on the street, "Straight or circular?" When you get something other than a date or a perplexed look, you've found a knitter.

10. Go to a department store and position yourself beside a display of standard-issue machine-knit sweaters. Put a sign on them that says 75 *percent off*. Watch for people who walk on by with nary a look.

two

YARN
and How
Not to Feel Guilty
About It

ONCE UPON A TIME, before I came to understand about yarn and the way things are, I felt sort of bad about my stash. Let's talk about when I first started dating my husband. The first few times I had him over I sort of "tidied up the yarn" a little. (You do know, don't you, that by "tidied up the yarn" I mean I stuffed it into bags and then into closets and cupboards and boxes and anywhere else I could to hide it?)

I didn't hide it all, though, partly because it's impossible and partly because I didn't want to hide the knitting thing entirely (it's like trying to keep secret that you occasionally sit under the back tree by the river singing long songs in a falsetto chicken voice). When you knit this much, it's such a big part of your personality that anyone who spends time with you is going to notice sooner or later. I just wanted an opportunity to charm him enough that when he found out about all the wool, he wouldn't back away from me slowly and then run screaming into the night. I wanted to let him in on the wonder that was me (and the stash) and, I hoped, by the time that he really understood how much yarn there was — and how little closet space he'd be getting — we'd be properly together and he'd have a legal obligation to stay . . . at least until I could whack a pair of hand-knit socks on him and make him mine forever.

MANAGING YOUR STASH

The whole time I was dating my husband, I kept quiet the extent of the yarn stash. I started to reveal it in stages, doses equal to the things that he revealed about himself. I discovered that he collected guitars, so I left the hall closet open one day. He showed me his set of antique

Yarn.

amplifiers (*Hint*: amps are big), and I showed him my set of vintage merino. He has a darkroom for his photography habit? What a coincidence. I have under-bed storage for my sock yarns. He has every issue of *Popular Electronics* from the 1950s? I mention that the funny manure smell he noted the other day might be the fleece in the basement.

Time passed and we came to share a home, and wouldn't you know it, he has never said a word. Part of it, I know, is that he respects me and my woolly choices, part of it is that he likes to see me happy, and part of it is that he knows what my reaction would be if he tried to tell me what to do with my stuff or how much I should have. I've returned the favor. It's taken a concerted effort, but it turns out that if you don't want to take any flack about the 17 half-knit sweaters on the dining room table, you just have to keep your mouth shut about the half-soldered recording console in the living room.

Marriage is about compromise.

> If you have to share space with a non-knitter, it's important to fully discover his or her hobbies. You're going to need ammunition when he or she finds out about the little accident you had when the yarn factory had a closeout sale.

BE DISCREET

You don't need to be so honest with the rest of the world. There's no reason for most of the ordinary people you run into — acquaintances, employers, psychiatrists — to know exactly what's going on with all the yarn or why you have so much. Seldom will you be understood, so discretion is the better part of valor. If you get caught, however, and someone unexpectedly discovers the full scope and extent of your yarn collection and is stunned into saying something, I offer the following retorts.

Someone says, **"You sure have a lot of yarn."**
You reply:

Response 1
"Thanks for noticing. It's been a big job and it's taken a long time, but I think I'm finally getting there."

Response 2
"This? No, no. This is just what I need for the week. The real collection is in my rental storage space."

Response 3
"Yeah, I know it's a lot. I really wanted a rock collection, but rocks are so heavy. This takes up a lot more room, but it sure is lighter."

Response 4
"Sorry, I couldn't hear you. All this yarn muffles the sound in here."

Response 5
"What? What yarn? These are my kittens."

If you have a lot of yarn, sometimes it's best just to leave it lying out in plain view. This causes a certain kind of "yarn-blindness," where your family will just stop seeing it. I realized this was possible when my daughter came into the living room (the living room that's practically buried in yarn) and said, "Hey, Mum? Do we have anything I could use like string?"

5
REASONS

Five Reasons to Keep a Stash

If anyone ever tries to make you feel guilty about your stash, there are several things you can point out.

1. Some people collect rocks or seashells. Enough said.

2. Yarn, if you get enough of it, can totally act as house insulation, helping to cool your house in the summer and hold in heat during the winter. It's almost irresponsible, in the face of global climate change, not to have a stash of yarn.

3. Wool is flame-retardant and what people in the fire business refer to as "self-extinguishing." If something self-extinguishing is exposed to a flame, when the flame is removed it will no longer burn. This means that (in my special

little world) having an extensive woolen stash is practically a safety thing. Remind me to call my insurance company to have my rates lowered.

4. Speaking of insurance, a stash protects against any number of emergencies. What if you lost your job and could no longer afford to buy yarn? What if you had to move to a remote mountain pass in Nepal and couldn't get to a yarn shop without a five-day hike? What if, out of the blue, huge felted woolen car cozies became popular and the world's supply of fiber was eaten up by the auto industry, causing wool scarcity and widespread panic among knitters everywhere? Better to be prepared. You never know when supply could dry up.

5. It's a way better alternative than drinking heavily or doing drugs, which is probably the way I'd spend my time if you took my knitting away.

yarn

CONSIDER THE ENTERTAINMENT VALUE

There's nothing wrong with buying stash. Many knitters feel guilty about this and attempt to curb their instincts to buy it all the time. If you were a carpenter, nobody would be surprised that you had a lot of wood. If you were a painter, we would fully expect there to be a houseful of paints. Provided that your inclination to buy yarn doesn't exceed your ability to pay for it, you really don't have a problem. If, however, you find yourself hocking furniture or skipping meals to get it, you may want to cut back a little.

> **Stash has a tendency to multiply. This is independent of your tendency to keep buying it, so don't bother resisting the urge. *Note:* This rule is true only of stash that's hanging around being decorative. Once you start to knit with it, it doesn't multiply . . . as any knitter who has run out of yarn a half-sleeve short of a sweater can testify.**

Really, the best way never to feel guilty about your stash is to think of yarn not as piles of recklessly purchased fiber (no matter how recklessly you purchased it) but instead as entertainment you've bought. By my reckoning, it's a pretty sweet deal.

A cheap ticket to see the musical *Les Misérables* in downtown Toronto costs about $50 (if you go alone) and lasts for three hours. That breaks down to $16.66 per hour for entertainment. A movie ticket is about $12 and if you're lucky, it'll be a long film. Let's say it's costing you $6 per hour to be entertained. My local video-rental place seems like a deal; I can get a movie for $5, which makes my cost per hour about $2.50.

I could take this further and look at CD and DVD collections, or, without picking on anyone in particular, my husband's affinity for antique audio equipment, or the cost of an Alaskan cruise, but the important point is this: A ball of sock yarn (a really nice one that will make two socks) costs about $16 if I get it on sale. If, then, I start to knit it up, it's going to take me (if I don't do a pattern or cables or anything at all that would slow me down) about 16 hours to complete. That makes my entertainment cost a whopping one buck an hour. If I do fancy socks, it's even more worthwhile. Let's say I put a fussy cable down the side of my socks. Well, now, that's going to take longer. It might take me 20 hours to knit those socks and now my entertainment is costing me just 80 cents an hour! Eighty cents? Who can feel guilty about spending 80 cents an hour when at the end of it you've not only scored yourself a whole pile of fun, but you also have a pair of socks?

Nobody gives you socks at the end of a musical, even if you buy the good seats.

FINDING A PLACE FOR IT ALL

I suffer under the delusion that I have my yarn "stored." Nothing could be further from the truth. In reality, all I have is my yarn — at the best of times —"contained." Once you admit your full and decent love affair with yarn

> **People often ask me my yarn-storage secrets. How I get so much yarn in such a small house without having to use it as carpet? Here's how. I break it up, I think outside the box (literally), I consider what to do with one skein at a time, and I never say die.**

and knitting, there'll come a time when the stash outgrows whatever box, bin, or basket you've been keeping it in. For me, this time came and went a long time ago . . . so I now have a really eclectic system.

I store yarn in "the yarn closets" and in plastic bins stacked in my office. I have several bookshelves full, and boxes, bins, and baskets throughout the house. My storage needs long ago surpassed my storage possibilities, and since then I've been a big fan of the "nook-and-cranny" system. I put yarn above and behind books on bookshelves, in cupboards in and around the other things that are there, and in any other wee space I can fit a skein.

DO YOU NEED TO LOSE A FEW POUNDS?

The concept of a yarn diet, as difficult as it may be to approach, is a fair one. One simply refrains from new yarn purchases, using only stash yarns, until the required number of yards or pounds has been "lost." I admit you have to be pretty far gone before you need this sort of drastic action . . . but you could be there. Let's get an assessment:

Question 1 If asked to move so that you were at least 10 feet away from yarn, you would be:

Ⓐ on the other side of the room.

B on the other side of the house.

C in the bathroom.

D outside on the sidewalk.

Question 2 How many people have mentioned your yarn "weight" to you in the last year?

A Nobody; how could anyone tell I have yarn?

B Only my husband, but he can be insensitive like that.

C Three, but they all live in this house, want closet space, and can't be trusted.

D Only my neighbor across the road, but that's because he can see in our windows. I got curtains.

Question 3 Has anyone ever told you that you have too much wool?

A Nope.

B Just my husband, but he can be insensitive like that.

C The lady who owns the yarn shop said something, but I think she's jealous.

D Not a single person. Then again, I haven't had much company since I gave up the couch for yarn space.

If your answers are mostly A: For the love of all things knitted, get to the yarn store. You have nothing.

If your answers are mostly B: Congratulations. You may enter at the amateur level. You don't need a diet, and can continue to spend freely in the yarn store, but you should consider some new shelving. You're going to need it.

If your answers are mostly C: You have, despite a substantial stash, no need to control your yarn intake. You should approach yarn with commonsense moderation and . . . oh, nuts. You're doomed. It's just a matter of time.

If your answers are mostly D: I don't want to use the "D" word, but you may want to consider choosing lighter-weight yarns more often, if you know what I mean.

STASH IDENTIFICATION: SMELLS LIKE MOHAIR TO ME

I'm forever finding yarn in the stash that I cannot identify. Despite my best efforts to be an organized and well-informed knitter, either I have weak moments or someone keeps breaking in and messing up my stash. Ball bands go missing (probably because I gave the yarn a test drive, then lost the ball band, rammed the yarn into a plastic bag, and then shoved it back into the stash, naked and unlabeled). Sometimes, though, because I have pangs of remorse and moments of insight, I'm compelled to write what's inside on the outside of the bag. In this case, it's likely that I'll go into the stash, discover a bag that says *wool/acrylic* on the bag and then stand around wondering about the possibilities.

They are:

- **The yarn is wool,** but when I wrote on the bag, there was another yarn in with it that was acrylic.
- **The yarn is acrylic,** but when I wrote on the bag, there was another yarn in with it that was wool.
- **The yarn is a wool/acrylic blend** (of course, I don't remember buying a wool/acrylic blend, but that doesn't mean much. I think I go into a yarn-buying trance under

Dear Inventor of Ziploc bags:

On behalf of the knitting community, I would like to take a moment to thank you for your contribution to our art. All over the world, knitters (and spinners) have yarn stashed away in the clear protective prison of a Ziploc bag. In my experience, the miracle of these resealable plastic wonders is multifold.

• They keep yarn dust-free. I refuse to discuss what it means that there are so many of us holding yarn for long enough that we need to contemplate layers of dust; I simply thank you.

• They keep yarn from unraveling into a tangle that complicates the relationship between knitters and yarn.

• They deter the scourge of the planet, the bane of our existence, the very heart of darkness... moths.

• They allow us to get more yarn in a closet, as when they're tightly packed, these plastic pouches make good, if slippery, bricks with which to build yarn walls.

I know you're probably unaware that this is a gift you have given us knitters, and I realize this use may be a surprise to you, in that you really seem to believe (if your advertising is any indication) that people are buying them to store food. Take it from me and the other 49,999,999 knitters in North America. Nobody has that much food. It's knitters.

Thankfully,
Stephanie

(Who would appreciate it if you would make a Ziploc bag big enough to hold a sweater's worth of wool, and solve the problem of the knitting needles poking holes in the plastic.)

extreme yarn conditions. I don't remember buying half of the stash. I don't let it bother me).

- **The yarn is neither wool, nor acrylic, nor a blend,** but is instead some yarn of a completely unrelated fiber content that got jammed into a leftover bag that I didn't notice had writing on it while I was trying to be a better person who keeps an orderly stash.

Naturally, because I am me, all attempts to organize my life or have a labeled stash and keep things in an orderly fashion are doomed to result in chaos and confusion, basically the opposite effect of what I was aiming for. In fact, instead of being a knitter who has this stash of power that makes sense and is accessible and inspiring, it turns out that I'm actually a knitter who inexplicably removes the ball bands from yarn and then jams the skeins into an enormous stash of other yarn that is remarkably similar, none of which I remember buying.

> It's worth noting that every single knitter who has ever wondered about the fiber content, yardage, or weight of a bandless ball thought, at the time that he put the ball into the stash, that he would remember what it was when he came across it again. Trust me. You won't.

In my defense (and clearly, I need defending, since I can't count the number of times I've found mystery yarn in the stash, with the label long abandoned or lost), I'm also a big thrift-store and sale-bin yarn buyer, and while that's frugal and admirable, it also breeds any number of bandless balls. I'm also a spinner with a lot of spinning friends, and gracious gifts of handspun don't come with labels.

There's stuff I need to know about my mystery yarn before I can knit it, and some simple yarn interrogation can tell a lot. Using a system of tests, measures, and cleverness, you can usually figure out pretty much what you have, even if you've lost the ball band.

Things can get a little odd for a yarn detective, so you might want to do some of your sleuthing while you're alone. Many valid yarn investigation methods might lead your nearest and dearest to believe you're a couple of skeins short of a sweater (if you know what I mean).

THE BURN TEST

There are three things you need to know about your suspect: what it's made of, what weight it is, and (heaven help you) how much there is. The most reliable way of figuring out what your yarn is made of is *the burn test.* This highly scientific way to torch your stash can tell you a lot about what you've got. *Warning:* I feel bad even mentioning this, because I know you're really smart, but I feel compelled to mention the obvious hazards of executing the burn test. First of all, have some water nearby. You never know what will burn, or how well. Second, conduct the burn test over a metal sink, not plastic. I'm not apologizing for what will happen if you drop a flaming piece of cotton into a meltable sink. Finally, I (as a woman who has set fire to far bigger chunks of the stash than she planned) suggest you burn small pieces of yarn and hold the pieces with tweezers or metal tongs (again, not plastic). Fire can travel faster than you think.

Ready? Get a piece of yarn, set a match to it, and watch closely.

Even after you have set fire to things, it may not be so simple to tell the differences between them.

Let's take a closer look:

• Cotton and linen burn similarly, but linen fibers are much longer than those of cotton. Pull out a few of the individual fibers and examine them. Are they long or short?

• Man-made fibers shrink from the flame; all-natural fibers do not.

• Rayon, because it's made from wood pulp, acts more like a natural fiber than a man-made one. It won't melt, but it will burn.

Fiber	Shrinks from the flame?	Smells like...
Wool	No	Burning hair or feathers
Cotton	No	Burning paper
Linen	No	Burning grass
Silk	No	Burning hair
Acrylic	Yes	Acrid or harsh odor
Nylon	Yes	Burning plastic
Rayon	Yes	Burning leaves

The flame...	Ignition	What's left behind
A small orange flame, difficult to keep burning; may simply smolder instead of burn	Doesn't ignite quickly and the flame goes out if wool is removed from the fire	A gummy ash forms along the burning edge of the wool, but when it's completely burned it leaves a crumbly ash
Large and steady yellow or amber flame	Lights right away and will have a glowing ember that travels after the flame is blown out	Small amount of soft gray ash
Large and steady	Slower than cotton	Soft gray ash
Tiny flame	Burns slowly but is harder to put out than cotton or linen	A black shiny ash that crumbles
A white-orange flame that burns quickly	Catches easily, will burn until extinguished	Hard ash
Flame has a blue base and orange tip	Melts, then burns	Hard ash
Orange	Lights and burns rapidly	Very little ash

THE BLEACH TEST

If the burn test hasn't helped you enough, try the bleach test. Put a small piece of the yarn in question in a dish of chlorine bleach, the kind you use for the laundry. Cotton and acrylic will stay put (though cotton will bleach white or yellow) but wool, silk, and other animal proteins (cashmere and alpaca, for example) will dissolve entirely in the bleach.

The bleach test and its effect on wool are important to remember the next time you want to get a blueberry stain off a really nice wool sweater that took you four months to knit.

THE FELT-ABILITY TEST

Wool (including mohair, alpaca, angora, and llama) felts, shrinks, and sticks to itself when you expose it to water, heat, and agitation. Silk, quiviut, and man-made fibers, on the other hand, do not. Take a length of the suspect yarn, squish it into a ball between your fingers, and then immerse it in hot soapy water. Squish, roll, and smoosh the yarn roughly for five minutes, then take it out and have a look. Try to pull apart your little ball. Is the yarn sticking to itself? Has it shrunk a little or begun to cling into a ball shape? If so, you probably have wool. If the yarn is still yarn, showing absolutely no inclination to stick to itself, you likely have acrylic, cotton, silk, a man-made fiber of another sort, or a superwash wool.

Superwash wool is wool that has been specially treated so that it will not felt, full, or shrink. If the suspect fiber seemed like wool when you burned or bleached it but it has now failed the felting test, consider the possibility

Knitting Rules!

that it is superwash. You may also consider the possibility that this whole thing is going to drive you nuts and then bury the skein in the backyard under a tree. We all understand.

IT SEEMS LIKE . . .

If, after burning, sniffing, bleaching, and guessing you still aren't sure what you have, go back to the stash and find something similar to what you think you have. If you think it's wool, put a wool yarn through the tests and see if it behaves like the suspect.

There is no test I know of (short of getting a microscope and an education in these matters) that will help you distinguish among different animal fibers. You can guess, by characteristics like elasticity and drape, but being able to reliably tell the difference between alpaca and llama is going to remain a challenge.

FIGURING WEIGHT

With experience, you're probably going to be able to tell if a yarn is chunky or worsted weight by giving it a little squeeze and, eventually, with a glance. If you don't have this experience, or if you're dealing with hand-spun, where it can be a little trickier, you could probably use a few hints.

The most reliable way to tell what you have is to swatch some of it, but I prefer using "wraps per inch" or WPI. This method is faster and leaves more knitting time. Find a ruler (sorry . . . I don't know where it is) and your yarn and plant yourself in a comfy chair. Wrap the yarn around the ruler — not too tight or you stretch the yarn;

not too loose or you can't measure properly. Just wrap, laying the yarn next to itself on the ruler so that you fill all the spaces between the strands, but don't squash them together. Find the marking for one inch on the ruler and count how many wraps of the yarn fit in that space. If you are an inconsistent wrapper or a really precise knitter, measure the wraps over a couple of inches and divide to get an average and consistent number.

HOW MUCH DO YOU HAVE?

Once you've figured out what your yarn is made of and what weight it is, the only thing left to wonder is "How

Wraps per Inch	Approximate yarn weight	Common gauge
More than 18	Floss or cobweb (occasionally referred to by non-knitters as "crazyville")	Variable, depending on effect desired
18	Lace weight	Variable
16	Fingering/sock yarn/ baby yarn	28 stitches to 4"/10 cm
14	Sport/light worsted/DK (double knitting)	24 stitches to 4"/10 cm
12	Worsted/aran	20 stitches to 4"/10 cm
10	Chunky/rug yarn	16 stitches to 4"/10 cm
8 or less	Bulky/superbulky	12 or less stitches to 4"/10 cm

much is in the ball?" (Well, there are also these questions: "Is it enough to make a sweater?" and "When will the world have peace?" but you know what I mean.)

Following are five ways to guesstimate how much you have of a particular yarn.

Method 1 **Get a McMorran balance.** This little gizmo is a kind of scale set to balance at a certain weight. You hang a piece of yarn on it, snip away at it until the arm balances, then measure the piece of yarn you have and multiply by 100. This tells you how many yards there are per pound. Then you weigh the skein and bob's yer uncle, you know how much yarn you have. (*Disadvantage:* You need to get a McMorran balance, and because it's mainly a spinner/weaver gadget, you may not be able to get one from your local yarn store.)

Method 2 **Get a yarn meter.** Clamp the meter onto a table in between the ball of yarn and your ball winder. Slide the yarn through the slot in the top of the thing, attach it to the ball winder, and start pulling the yarn through the meter by winding it on the ball winder. The yarn passes through little rollers in the middle that count off yards or meters, and displays how much has passed through. (*Disadvantage:* Requires a ball winder, and because most have a digital display, they stop working if you happen to spill coffee on them.)

Method 3 **Cut 10 yards of yarn from the ball** and take the piece and that ball over to the post office. Get someone there to weigh the 10 yards. (If your post office is sort of cranky about your knitting problems, you could buy a scale that measures down to half a gram.) Now you know how much 10 yards weighs, and you can weigh the ball and do the math to figure out the rest. (*Disadvantage:* This method is not as accurate as the meter or balance, and it relies on your ability to do math. If you have trouble with that kind of thing, you may want another option.)

Method 4 **Wind the yarn around a skein winder** like a niddy noddy, or use the back of a chair if you don't have one. Then measure the distance around the chair, count the number of times it went around, and then do the math. This is a good option for the knitter who has time but no tools. (*Disadvantange*: It's as tedious as explaining the phone rules to a 16-year-old girl, and just as time-consuming.)

Method 5 **Measure it against a yardstick.** This is probably the most accurate, least technical method, but unless you have a really short skein of yarn, it's only slightly more fun than shaving your head with a rusty razor.

YARN TYPES

I've never met a yarn I didn't like. Well, let me take that back. I've never met a yarn I didn't like for *something*. All yarns have a purpose (even if you can't imagine it). I admit, if you are a traditional lace knitter, then the purpose of bulky neon yellow acrylic might be lost on you, but I assure you, there's some other knitter standing in another yarn shop somewhere else in the world holding your treasured lace weight in her hand and thinking, "What on earth would you do with this thread?" There are knitters who never knit with wool and knitters who use only cotton. There are knitters who've told me that silk smells funny (I refuse to entertain that) and knitters who find mohair too fuzzy. There are also self-professed "fiber snobs" who use only natural fibers and frown on acrylic, but they are canceled out by the acrylic fans who are laughing their rear ends off when the snobs get a moth infestation. Then there are the knitters who know this:

All yarn is here for a reason. No one fiber (or sort of knitter) is *morally* superior to another.

If you can't stand on the moral high ground for choosing the right fiber (or at least, I hope you won't), then how do you pick? Advantages and disadvantages. Think of your potential yarn as a date and write yourself a little "pro-and-con" chart, just like you did when you were a teenager and had to make a decision.

Before you go making a blanket statement about a fiber, like "Wool is itchy" or "Acrylic is crap," keep in mind that fibers may have changed since the last time you met them. Acrylic is no longer (not necessarily, anyway) the sort of plastic extruded stuff you remember from the 1970s. Some of it is downright elegant, soft, and — in the case of new microfiber technology — intriguing and unique. On the other side of the fence, wool isn't necessarily (though you can sure find it if you look for it) the scratchy stuff your winter long johns were made out of, either. Go to the yarn shop and take an open mind with you.

WOOL

Wool is the vanilla of the fiber world. It's the work-horse of knitting and we know why. Wool is warm when it's wet, emits heat as it dries (damn, that's cool), and is a renewable resource. It's also naturally flame-retardant, making it a great choice for blankies and clothes for kids. There's tough wool that wears like iron and wool softer than butter. There's superwash wool that goes in the washer and drier and wool that doesn't go in the washer and drier, making it good for felting. Wool is forgiving and elastic, retains its shape well, and can be persuaded (by blocking) to take on a new shape. Wool is the fiber not of choice, but of choices.

One very good reason to knit with wool is its malleability. Wool stretches and shrinks, and, generally speaking, bends to the will of the knitter very nicely. If you are, like me, an "imprecise" knitter, this characteristic of wool will suit you, as it forgives mistakes and unevenness like no other fiber.

Wool is moth food and if you have a big stash, you can't put that much moth food in one place and not expect them to flutter to the buffet. Also, wool felts. Although I presented this as an advantage above, that was when I was assuming you wanted it to. When it happens by accident, it's a disadvantage. Wool takes — much like the people who will wear it — a little care when washing.

COTTON

Cotton is a natural fiber, cool (cooler than wool) to wear, and a wonderful option for knitters who live in

southern climes. (I understand that my affection for wool probably seems silly to Hawaiian knitters.) It's durable, comes in many wonderful and vibrant colors because it takes dye well, and is almost without exception soft and approachable. Like wool, cotton is available at a range of prices.

Cotton is inelastic, and things that depend on elasticity, like socks and ribbing, are going to need to be either abandoned or adapted (sometimes by adding elastic) to make them work. Cotton can also be quite heavy, something to consider if you're talking about a size large cabled sweater that you expect to keep its shape. (Ask me how I know.)

ACRYLIC

Acrylic yarns tend to be less expensive than their natural-fiber counterparts and are not moth food. Acrylic yarn is easy to find, and most acrylics are also easy care, happily swinging in and out of the laundry without so much as a nod to the risk of felting.

Acrylic yarn can't be blocked the way wool can and, with few exceptions, is less elastic and forgiving than wool. Acrylic yarn doesn't breathe or absorb moisture either, and although it doesn't felt, it can be ruined with heat, so follow the label instructions for washing and don't ever iron it. Remember, too, that acrylic is especially dangerous in a fire: it melts, burns, and sticks. This makes it an especially poor choice for anything you plan to put on a child at night.

CRAP IN, CRAP OUT

This was a phrase we took to using when the kids were little. It meant that if you fed a kid a chocolate bar and four cookies, let her miss her nap, and then sat her down for 30 minutes of TV, you shouldn't have been surprised when she spent all 30 minutes trying to kick her sister in the head because "she won't stop looking at me."

Knitting is like that. (Not that it tries to kick you in the head, though I understand that if you've recently experienced a knitting loss, it may feel that this particular metaphor is too close for comfort.) In knitting, your end product can be only as good as your starting place. Crap in, crap out.

There are exceptions to this: knitters who can start with the biggest pile of crap and have it turn out to be a breathtaking beauty. It's like they have the ability to look deep into a yarn's eyes and see its unique charms and then imagine how best this particular yarn can be brought into the light and be all that it can be. It's a gift, and not many of us have it. Most of us, given crap yarn, are going to knit crap. Whenever I meet one of these rare knitters who doesn't, I'm always torn between falling on the ground at her feet and begging her to tell me all she knows, and locking her in my basement and never speaking of her again.

Julia Child said when it comes to wine for cooking, you should use the best you can afford. I beg you now to do the same with yarn. Buy the best you can afford. The stuff you make is your legacy, and your time is really worth it.

THE POTENTIAL OF YARN

It's difficult to write, once you're done with the technical aspects of yarn, about the real stuff you need to know about it: the soul of yarn, its magic, and why, beyond it being the material we need to practice the art of knitting, we love it. I could wax poetic for hours about the softness, the colors, the textures . . . the things I like about yarn. But none of that really gets to the meat of it.

In the end, the reason we fill our houses with it, visit it in yarn shops, speak of it in glowing terms, and hoard it with passion is that it is pure potential. Every ball or skein of yarn holds something inside it, and the great mystery of what that might be can be almost spiritual. These six balls of wool could be a shawl my mum puts around her shoulders when she's cold, or maybe it's a blanket a friend wraps her baby in. Maybe that baby takes a shine to it and it becomes his beloved companion blankie, comforting him for years and years. Maybe it's a sweater that my daughter is wearing the day she gets her first kiss, and from then on my yarn is a part of her memory of that day. Maybe, just maybe, those six balls are a scarf and hat that get tucked away for years and long after I'm gone someone pulls them out and says, "Remember how Grammy was with all the wool? Remember how she knit all the time?" fingering the soft wool and pondering who I was and what I did while I was here.

It's a mystery, each ball of yarn . . . and I don't know what each one is going to be or what life it will take when I finally set needles to it. But each one will be something I made with my own two hands. This yarn, then — my whole big sweeping stash — *is the stuff of dreams.*

three

Know Your
STUFF

KNITTING ISN'T JUST ABOUT THE YARN and the projects. As the friends and families of knitters will tell you (as they look for a clear space to sit), knitting comes with a lot of stuff. From needles to patterns to tape measures, these bits and pieces are as necessary as yarn to our craft, and have a variety and volume that matches any yarn stash.

The wise knitter (that would be you; since my knitting stuff is a disaster) organizes her stuff, keeps it handy, and knows how to use it. The unwise knitter (that would be me) rummages around, makes do with what she's got, and still has a pretty good time. Part of the occasionally bitter song and the often wonderful surprise of knitting is that your projects don't always work out as happily as an after-school movie. There are simply too many variables for there to be no surprises, but over time I've learned that understanding your stuff (even if your stuff isn't very good stuff) improves the odds of getting a predictable knitting outcome.

When it comes to my spare time (and my working time too, now that I think about it, as I work at writing knitting books), it would appear that I'm a woman of limited intelligence. It's not that I consider myself unintelligent, I'm pretty sure I'm about as smart as the next knitter. Rather, I mean that the scope of my intelligence is limited. I know a great deal about just one thing. I don't know anything about barometric pressure; I can't make sushi; really, all I care about deeply (my family and spiritual life aside) is knitting.

I suspect that many of you are the same, and, considering the relative simplicity of knitting, that it occupies a space in your heart, mind, and home that's larger than expected. This limited intelligence, or focus, makes the processes of knitting matter a great deal. Knitting is simple, and this means that once you have the basics of knit and purl down cold, attention to detail starts to matter and knitters tend to get uptight about smooth knitting needles, lost gauges, errant tape measures, and the accuracy of patterns. It turns out that if you're a Knitter (note the capital *K*) and you've taken up the process of knitting at all seriously, you'll be with me in thinking that figuring out the best kind of needle for you makes a lot of sense.

KNITTING NEEDLES

Without knitting needles, we would simply be surrounded by piles of beautiful string. Needles come, infuriatingly, in several kinds of sizes, materials, and types and if you're like me, you'll no doubt decide you need them all. There could be a therapy group for knitters driven over the edge by a circular needle with a sloppy join that snags their lace weight, and an entire evening could be spent berating a needle that lacks a tip pointy enough to do a "knit three together through the back loops." How, then, to choose among the hundreds of needles currently littering your home?

SIZES

Knitting needles come in sizes that indicate their diameter. These sizes are measured mainly by three systems (four, if you count my personal system of losing all my needle gauges and having to roll needles between my fingers and make a guess). There is the metric "mm" system, the most common in the world and, to my way of thinking, the best. Each needle size is actually its diameter in millimeters, a concept brilliant in its simplicity. There is the U.S. system, in which each needle is measured and then assigned a number. In this system, the smallest number is the smallest size and so forth. It's still a good system, though used only in the United States, so if you're a knitter from another country, or a knitter who likes patterns from another country, you're going to have to get down with the metric system. The third system is the old United Kingdom one. This is like the U.S. one, except the smallest numbers are the biggest needles.

It pays to think outside of your own country. Once upon a time I had a nifty Irish sweater pattern. It called for chunky wool, and I had fished the appropriate yarn out of the stash. Glancing at the pattern, I saw that it called for size 4 needles. It seemed odd, but I grabbed my size 4s and attempted to get gauge. An hour later, when I had just about broken my wrists and produced a piece of knitting so dense that I thought about marketing it as a bulletproof vest, I thought about the conversion chart. I, naturally, being Canadian, had thought the pattern referred to the metric size 4. Feeling quite clever, I fished out my U.S. size 4s only to

One of the beautiful things about knitting, and oh, there are so many, is that it can be done with very little. An equally good time can be had by the knitter with a pair of old aluminum straights or a collection of gold-plated circulars. It's all about doing it your way. Admittedly, you're still going to want to run yourself through with whatever needle you've chosen when you can't find the needle gauge for the 14th time, but that's universal, and unrelated to needle type.

Needle Sizes

Metric	U.S.	UK
10	15	000
9	13	00
8	11	0
7.5	—	1
7	—	2
6.5	10.5	3
6	10	4
5.5	9	5
5	8	6
4.5	7	7
4	6	8
3.75	5	9
3.5	4	—
3.25	3	10
3	—	11
2.75	2	12
2.25	1	13
2	0	14
1.75	00	15

All needles don't come in all sizes. For example, the metric system has two sizes between the U.S. size 11 and 10.5. If you get a pattern calling for something you don't have, don't lose your cool. One of knitting's charms is that often, close enough is good enough. If you want to get uptight about it, though, there's always mail order to get needles with an international flair.

Knitting Rules!

realize that they were even smaller. Frustrated, I then did what any other knitter would do. I used whatever needle it took to get gauge . . . and complained bitterly to my knitting friends about the error in the pattern.

Laughing, they openly mocked me, and then showed me a chart with the UK sizes on it. Now, before I slag any pattern for being wrong, I try to remember that I don't live in the only country in the world.

It seems pathetic to list the conversion chart for these three types here again, since I'm confident that this is the ten-millionth time someone has written it down, but I can never find one when I need it, and until the world is run by a knitter government that standardizes this sort of thing, well, you're going to need one. Be warned that when knitters run the world, coming up with one consistent system of needle sizing is going to be the first thing we address.

A STRAIGHT PATH?

Once you've come to understand knitting needle sizing, you'll have to weigh in on straight versus circular needles. This one simple point (or two) is probably the issue of greatest contention among knitters. It really doesn't take long for a knitter to make up her mind about her preference, and most make no bones about an inflexible opinion.

Straight needles are:

- Less expensive.
- Readily available and easy to find. Even a dollar store usually carries them.

- Used only for knitting things that aren't circular. (I know that seems obvious, but I'm trying to be thorough.)
- Possibly faster, depending on your knitting style. "Armpit knitters," or those who tuck one needle under an arm, are among the fastest in the world, and they use straight needles exclusively, since tucking a circular under your arm leads to cramping, knitting failure, and an odd chicken-like posture.
- Traditional, and I really like that. There's a certain something about knitting with the same tools that people knit with centuries ago. Circulars are relatively new on the scene, and I like the idea of connecting with so many knitters who came before me. (This fantasy is blown right out of the water if you're knitting with shiny-colored aluminum needles, but I can ignore that.)
- Easy to store neatly in just about anything — a drawer, a bag, a vase, down the side of a chair.
- Useful as a personal defense system in a pinch.

Circular needles are:
- A little more expensive.
- Slightly less likely to be lost down a crack on the bus or to roll away from you loudly in a dark and quiet movie theater. (Not that I would know from experience.)

If you're ever in a yarn store full of knitters and decide (for reasons I can't imagine) you'd like to start the knitting-shop equivalent of a bar fight, take a deep breath and make the following statement: *"Straight [or circular] knitting needles are stupid."* Then stand back and watch the wool fly.

- Useful for flat (back and forth) or circular knitting. Thus making it possible (and I hate to admit this, my love for straight needles being as pure as it is) for you to use just circular needles your whole knitting life.
- More difficult to store.
- Tied together so you can't lose one. (Until you've lost a straight mid-project, you really don't understand the advantage of this.)
- Available in more sizes, since there are two parts to the sizing (the diameter of the needles and the length of the cord) and both measurements matter. Hence, you may need to purchase more of them.

Circular needles come in an assortment of lengths, as — at least when you're using them to knit circularly you need a needle that is a shorter length than the diameter of your total stitches. (There are exceptions to this, and if you must know, they involve using two circulars or one very, very long one.)

When you're buying a circular needle, know that the length is the distance from tip to tip, not the length of the cord. I learned this the hard way, and have a whole drawer of wrong-length needles to prove it.

DOUBLE-POINTED NEEDLES

These are a fancy animal. They're straight needles that you use to knit circularly. They scare the daylights out of a lot of new knitters, who see four or five needles sticking out of a sock in progress and immediately imagine that managing five needles has to be more complicated than using two. All I have to say to newcomers to double points is this: Remember that no matter how many needles are present, you only use two at a time. Be not afraid.

Double-pointed needles are shockingly useful. They're good for small tubes, like the arms of a baby sweater; they're indispensable for making I-cord; and they come in handy for picking locks, fending off other knitters at a yarn sale, and retrieving things (like stitch markers) from small spaces (like heating grates).

If you're having a really good time with a needle someone else (or maybe everyone else) says is crap, ignore the warnings. You can like crap if it works for you.

WHAT ARE YOUR NEEDLES MADE OF?

Knitters don't get serious only about circular or straight; there's also the deeply divisive matter of needle material. Needles come made of all kinds of stuff, and they all have their advantages. For the longest time I knit exclusively with cheap aluminum-colored needles. I liked how cheerful they were; the way I could match the needle color to the yarn; and how sharp, fast, and inexpensive they were. These days I'm more likely to match my needle type to my yarn type, and though I miss the thrill of putting hot pink yarn on blue needles, I must admit I'm pretty keen on the way mohair clings to the wooden ones.

It's possible to buy crappy needles of every sort. There are wooden needles that break or splinter, there are metal needles that aren't smooth, and plastic ones with a point so blunt you couldn't poke a hole in Jell-O with them. The advantages of each type refer only to needles of reasonable quality. As with yarn, buy the best quality you can afford, and don't tar a whole group of needles until you've bought (or borrowed) them in their finest form.

WOOD

Needles made of wood are available in many different flavors of tree. Common woods are birch, beech, maple, and bamboo, though for a price you may choose warm, elegant rosewood or hard, exotic ebony. Knitters who love wooden needles say they're quiet, warm, pleasantly organic, beautiful to look at, and improve with age. Knitters say they're smooth without being too slick, making them very, very good for really slippery yarns that don't want to stay put on the needles and for complex lacework where control matters.

Knitters who don't like wooden ones say that they're "slow" (the grip that helps with slippery yarn can work against you if your yarn is not slippery) and that they're quite breakable. It's true that some kinds are stronger than others, but virtually nothing will save a wooden needle if you sit on it. (I, having sat on both fragile and sturdy needles, advocate wood for the clumsy knitter. It hurts less.) Every once in a while you hear about a knitter whose wooden needle broke during normal use, but it's more common for either a tight knitter or a knitter experiencing an unusual amount of stress. (For the purposes of this examination, I don't consider "normal use" to be flinging them on the floor in a fit of rage over a stitch pattern that you've screwed up for the fourth time since dinner. Normal use and common use are not interchangeable.)

METAL

Metal needles range from the plain steel and aluminum ones all the way up to nickel- or gold-plated needles with the appealing brand name Turbo. (This always makes my husband laugh; since he imagines race cars and rocket engines and knitters who need flameproof jackets to protect them from the exhaust emitted by the needles. He was disappointed to discover that they look like ordinary, if extra-shiny, knitting needles.)

People who love metal needles say that they're slippery, quick, and strong; that they tend to have the sharpest points — a real boon to knitters doing a lot of cables; and that they are (with the exception of the Turbo variety) the least expensive of all. Knitters who like them say that they're good for sticky wool but far too slick for mohair or lace and that they're the sturdiest of all needles. I can vouch for this, having managed to snap all varieties of needles except the metal ones. (I don't try to do this; it's a talent.)

Knitters who don't care for metal needles say they're cold, heavy, and inflexible and that the slipperiness makes for dropped stitches. Me? I love them.

PLASTIC

These vary almost too much to discuss effectively. If you're thinking of those old, blunt, floppy needles that were as smooth as bricks . . . well. You can still buy those, but there are needle manufacturers that have elevated them way beyond that. There are plastic needles with a metal core to make them stronger; plastic needles with special tips; transparent colored needles that turn my 14-year-old's crank pretty hard; and plastic needles that, in short, do not suck. Overall, today's plastic needle is flexible, warm, light, and probably the best option to give a five-year-old boy just learning to knit. (Having been poked with several kinds of knitting needle by a five-year-old boy just learning to knit, I can vouch for this.)

CASEIN NEEDLES

These are warm, light, and slightly flexible. Casein needles are made from milk protein and, as such, three things are true about them.

1. They share many of the advantages as plastic, but are a natural material.

2. Many strict vegetarians or vegans eschew them because they are an animal product.

3. They taste (not that I'm suggesting eating them) very, very bad, so don't hold one in your mouth.

OTHER MATERIALS

Knitting needles continue to surprise me. Some come with moral problems, like ivory, tortoiseshell, and walrus tusk needles, all of which are now illegal to buy or produce. If you have some, passed down from a knitter who didn't know better or a time when they weren't illegal, guard them with your life; they will not pass this way again and are an interesting footnote in knitting's history. There are bone needles, which may be an issue for some knitters. (Frankly, they creep me out.) There are beautiful glass needles, more for show than go, and hand-painted wooden ones. For a mere $1,800 you can have solid gold needles, but I shudder to think what you'd be compelled to do when you inevitably lost one.

10
REASONS

The Top Ten Reasons to Carry a Knitting Bag

1 Done right, you'll always have everything you need. This works only if you regard the knitting bag as a sacred carrier of knitting notions that never go anywhere except in the bag. You take something out, you put it back in. (This was one of the barriers to effective knitting bag use. I would take out the tape measure while I was home, because I couldn't find one of my 72 others, and fail to put it back in. It would then enter the tape measure—sucking void that is my home and I'd never find it again.) Do not, I repeat, *do not* put the stuff on the kitchen counter. This way lies madness.

2 If there were some sort of emergency, like an earthquake or a house fire, you could pick up your knitting bag from its spot by the door and flee with it into the night. I bet you'll be the only person at the shelter with something to do.

3 If you put everything you need to accomplish the project in the bag when you begin the project, you'll never again lose six hours and 35 minutes of your life shredding the stash looking for the last ball of blue merino you need to finish the sweater.

4. Unlike when you jam a project into your purse, you won't need to spend your knitting time untangling lace weight from house keys.

5. The breath mints you keep in your purse won't have yarn fuzz on them. Just regular purse lint.

6. Your 2 mm DPNs won't poke a hole in your juice box. (This is more likely than you think. Before I succumbed to a knitting bag, I had to give up grape juice. It really stains.)

7. You'll have more room to carry knitting stuff, as it doesn't have to compete with your purse contents.

8. You can take only your knitting bag into the yarn shop when you're going in to knit with your friends or to get help with a project. This means that when you inevitably decide to buy yarn, you will have to go back to the car to get your wallet. This won't prevent you from buying yarn, but at least it adds exercise to your day and may slow up impulse buying.

9. It gives you another place to keep yarn.

10. Knitting bags have a sturdy inside layer to keep sharp knitting needles from poking through. The same apparently can't be said for my purse, which always resembles a dangerous steel porcupine.

STUFF KNITTERS CARRY AROUND

I know this knitter . . . now, usually I change the names of knitters when I write about them, but that's because it's so often a story about disaster, a failure to think ahead, or them getting their arse kicked by a project in the worst way, and it's only fair not to give their real names. This time, though, because I'm going to speak of this knitter in the most glowing terms, this time I'm going to be honest and tell you that this knitter's name is Diane.

Diane is the rarest of knitters. Whenever I hung out with her, no matter where we were, Diane had not only everything she needed (something I admire, as I never have everything I need), but everything anybody else might need as well. You could be anywhere with Diane — a coffee shop, a yarn store, the bus — and no matter what you needed for your knitting, Diane had it. You would realize that you'd forgotten your scissors and be reconciling yourself to the fact that you were going to have to gnaw off a strand of mohair and whammo — Diane would pull scissors out of her bag. Wondering if you had knit eight inches? Diane had a tape measure. Grafting a toe? Diane had a darning needle and a small card outlining the steps. It was incredible. She was, and remains, the best-prepared knitter I ever met.

The best knitting bag is sturdy, is large enough to hold a pattern without folding it, has large handles so you can sling it over your shoulder, has lots of little pockets to hold your knitting notions, and — most important — holds more than one project. The prepared knitter has choices.

Considering my chronic lack of preparedness, and the yarn inevitably stuck between my teeth because I couldn't find my scissors, I've taken careful note of what Diane carried with her.

THE MODEL KNITTING BAG

The bag itself is worth mentioning. It took me a long time to come around to the idea of carrying a knitting bag. I'm more of a backpack kind of gal, and it was many, many years before I saw the wisdom of carrying a bag specifically for knitting. The advantages of putting together a knitting bag are multifold.

WHAT SHOULD BE INSIDE

A measuring tape. You can't have too many; they have a tendency to flee the scene. Tuck one (or two) in your knitting bag, but have a dozen or so scattered around the house to improve your odds.

A notebook and pencil. Use them to jot down what row you were on, the phone number of the nice knitter you met in the shop, and any alteration you made to the pattern. (Trust me: A scrap of paper or the back of a receipt does not suffice.)

A photocopy of your pattern. Copyright law allows you to make a working copy for personal use. This is a good idea. You can scrawl notes all over it and when (not if . . .) you lose it, it's not as heartbreaking as losing a whole pattern book. Additionally, the fates are kinder to photocopies. The knitting goddess can never quite resist giving you a smack and seeing how you'd cope without a pattern. If you were Diane, you would also have the pattern tucked into a plastic page protector, but this is advanced level.

A crochet hook. This is a big help for picking up dropped stitches, working provisional cast-ons, and fishing your DPN out of a crack in the sofa.

An extra set of needles in the size you're using. You know why.

A set of needles a size larger and a size smaller than the ones you're using. You'll be grateful for these when you realize a desperate gauge error kind of late in the game and you're in a place where you can't buy more needles. (When I run the world, there will be no place where you cannot buy needles, but I digress.)

A needle gauge. This invaluable little piece of plastic or metal can help you with three things: converting needle sizes among metric, UK, and U.S. sizes; figuring out if you have four matching DPNs; and measuring things when you have no tape measure, since they usually have a small ruler on one side. See *measuring tape* above.

A darning needle. This is a good one. Other stuff you can rig if you need to, but there's really no way to sew a seam without a darning needle.

Stitch holders and coil-less safety pins. I won't insult you by telling you what stitch holders are for. Coil-less safety pins function the same way; they hold an individual stitch or two; mark a row for decrease; or remind you which is the right side of your work if you're using fuzzy yarn, doing garter stitch, or combining knitting and a cocktail.

Stitch markers. These are invaluable for newcomers to lacework. Stitch markers make the divisions between repeats obvious, mark a line of decreases, or tell you when you are halfway across large rows — very motivating.

Sticky notes. The unsung heroes of knitting, I use them to mark where I'm at on a pattern or move them up a chart as I work it. I used to cross out or highlight rows, but that system has its drawbacks if you have to yank back six rows.

Row counter. This little device is a spool-shaped bit of plastic that either fits on your knitting needle or dangles from it. It usually has two numbered dials you can turn to count rows 01 through 99. Darned handy for working stitch patterns that are different on every row or patterns that would have you work "25 rows before you begin shaping."

A row counter beats the pants off my seemingly brilliant system, which involved setting out 25 candies and eating one at the end of every row. When the candy was gone, I had worked 25 rows. Problems emerge when on a knitting marathon and working 245 rows (in which case I ended up nauseated), or if you have children or a spouse with a sweet tooth (in which case all of your knitting ends up oddly short as your counters go missing).

THE ART OF THE KNITTER'S NOTEBOOK

If there was just one thing I would have you carry around, just one thing you could have with you that would save you more pain and knitting heartache and give you back simple happiness and peace of mind, just one thing I would take with me if my house burst into flames and I had time (after saving the people; you know I would take the people first . . . the people *and* that skein of blue silk I love), it would be the knitting notebook. Mine isn't anything fancy or special — it's just a spiral-bound book of graph paper. I carry it with me whenever I'm knitting, and we have come to have a deep and meaningful relationship.

It's because of the knitting notebook that I can make two socks the same without driving myself insane as I squint and curse. I make notes of how many stitches I cast on for the right mitten so I can do the same for the left. It's because of this notebook that I can remember how it was that I changed the top of the first sleeve and how to do the same to the second one. The knitting notebook is where I write all of my knitting math and make notes of the gauge and needles I'm using, and it's where I note how many meters of yarn I need for that shawl I'm thinking about, if I see something good in the yarn shop, I can get the right amount. Mine has graph paper so I can draw simple charts for Fair Isle and intarsia, or invent (sometimes by accident) a new pattern for lace.

The notebook also holds invaluable notes like "Susan says the new Smithers merino is crap," and "Sale in yarn shop on June 21." The knitting notebook is especially useful to multitasking knitters; if you get in the habit of writing down how many of the 12 sleeve decreases you've done on the blue sweater, you don't have any trouble when you pick it up again seven months (or years) from now, after you got distracted by three shawls and a pair of socks.

PROJECT JOURNALS

Some knitters take it even further and these days they're my heroes. They're the ones who keep a project journal, a sort of scrapbook where they record the details of the project, the pattern used, a snip of the yarn, one of the ball bands, what they thought of that yarn, what changes they made to the pattern, the measurements of the finished item, and the recipient. With the overachieving knitter, there's also a photo of the finished garment.

When I was a young mother with three daughters under five, there was this other mother down the street. She had three kids, too, and we should have felt a certain kinship, sailing along as we were in similar boats, but she drove me nuts. This woman (whom we shall call "Martha" for the sake of this story) kept perfect house. Martha never had to give the cat a can of tuna because she'd forgotten to buy cat food. She never sent her kids to school with mud stains on their pants and told them to tell other people it was "paint from arts and crafts." She certainly never took home a screaming kid from the park

Project journals are to be revered. Regard them with respect. Don't mock the knitter who keeps one, but know in your heart that the occasional hostility you feel (and the secret hope you have that she runs short of yarn) comes from your own feelings of inadequacy and guilt over that episode with the green cardigan when you accidentally knit the left front from one pattern and the right from another. That never happens to the journal-keeping knitters.

for whacking some other kid. Her house was immaculate and her spices were alphabetized. (She wasn't a knitter.) I hated her. She made me feel like I was doing a crappy job.

I can admit, now that I'm mature and accepting, that I sometimes have some negative feelings about these journal-keeping knitters. I feel about them (in my weaker moments) the way I used to feel about Martha. I'm trying to be a better person.

PAPER, AND ITS PERILS

For most knitters, myself included (though things may be worse at my house, as I have a love of books as well as of knitting), there is only one thing we struggle to manage as much as yarn. It isn't tape measures, notions, or scissors — those manage themselves by disappearing at regular intervals to keep us from being overwhelmed. It's patterns, knitting books, and magazines. (I think it's ironic that a knitting-book author is about to suggest ways to manage the problem; I'm part of the problem and it's therefore doubtful that I can be part of the solution.) I'm certainly — being a knitting-book writer — not going to suggest that buying fewer of them is the answer. I do, however, have some ideas.

PATTERNS

I keep all patterns. I don't know why. Say I've just finished a sweater where the pattern had a thousand mistakes, was poorly written, drove me insane, and produced, in the end, a sweater that lacked style and grace exactly the way a bag of hammers does. Instead of doing the logical thing, which is taking it into the living room, standing before the roaring fireplace, and, knowing fully and completely that I will never, ever knit that pattern again (nor would I wish it on my worst knitting enemy), casting it into the flames along with a few choice words about the designer and the horse she rode in on. Instead of this, I'll take it upstairs and put it on a shelf.

I'm compelled to keep it. It's a knitting pattern and therefore, even if it makes me want to stick knitting needles in my eyes, it has inherent value and I have to put it on the shelf. I will never knit it again. I will never lend it to another knitter. In all likelihood, I will curse its presence on the bookshelf when I run out of room for other good patterns, but I will keep it.

I'm not proud of this, but I know I'm not alone. So, for those of us who can't part with patterns, here are a few ways to store them:

Method 1 **Get a stack of file folders.** Label one *socks,* another *hats,* one *sweaters — kids,* and so on. Put the folders on the shelf. When you go upstairs to put a pattern on the shelf (or instead of making a stack of them on the bedside table), file it in the appropriate folder. This is also where you put the 8,000 patterns you've printed off the Internet. Start early. If you're an established knitter who adopted the "stack" system early, I don't know what to suggest for you, except maybe paying some 10-year-old to sort them. Don't attempt to convert the system yourself unless you're the "Martha" sort of person described earlier in this chapter. (That's pretty funny actually, since if you were the Martha sort of person, you wouldn't have had the stack system in the first place.)

Method 2   **Some knitters (though I'm not one of them, and this works only with patterns you haven't used yet) put the pattern in the stash** beside the yarn for the project. This works pretty well. It means you have to manage only the pattern you're finished with (and most knitters have more patterns they "are going to use" than they "have used"), and has the bonus of reminding you what your intentions were for the 12 skeins of green wool anyway.

Method 3   **For the "Martha" knitters out there, you can go completely over the top and employ a system of binders and plastic page protectors** and file the patterns by type, weight, and designer the minute you finish with them or even bring them into the house. What I really like about this system is that when (not if) you spill coffee, tea, or red wine on a pattern, you can just wipe it off the plastic page protector and still read the chart.

> **Your own knitting library is inevitable. Here's how it begins. You finish your first knitting project and you need to find a place to put the pattern. You go over to the bookshelf and put the pattern there next to some ordinary books. Done. It's over. You've just begun a long slide down a slippery slope.**

MAGAZINES

The last time I was in the bookstore by my house I wandered over to the magazine rack and counted seven different knitting magazines on the shelf. I had none of them. Now you can't just haul off and buy seven knitting magazines . . . you need to be a little discriminating.

I have criteria that I apply to my knitting magazines to help keep buying binges under control.

I purchase only a knitting magazine if at least one of the following is true:

1. There is a pattern that I really like and will likely knit.
2. There is an article that describes a technique or approach I find intriguing.
3. There is a pattern for a garment that I would never knit but find inspirational.
4. There is a pattern or article from a designer or writer I like.
5. I have every other issue and don't want to break up the set.

That time, I left with seven magazines. I always leave with seven. I put them on the shelf by the books.

BOOKS

I admit to owning a lot of knitting books. I'm not going to offer any ideas for managing them, buying fewer, or making good use of them. I suggest you put them on a shelf (or 10) together in one room (to make it easier to find the one you want) and celebrate them every chance you get.

I'm even going to encourage you to get more books by recommending that every knitter's library contain the following five types of books:

Type 1 At least one thorough, decent book on technique. You want a book in which you can look up Kitchener stitch, backstitching a seam, which decrease leans left, and tells you how to cast on and off several different ways. You can't always call your knitting friends for help at four in the morning on Christmas day. (Well, you can, and they might even understand, but the book will save you from needing to.)

Type 2 Stitch dictionaries. These books are pure inspiration. Filled cover to cover with ideas and patterns for wildly interesting ways to knit, stitch dictionaries are to knitters what the notes of the scale are to a piano virtuoso. Owning stitch dictionaries lets you add a lace cuff to a baby sweater, a cable to a sock, or to come up with 37 styles of ribbing.

Type 3 Books with patterns for simple, plain garments in shapes you like. These patterns will, as you move through your knitting life, become the templates for stuff that springs free of your imagination. A good sweater pattern can lead to 20 brilliant sweaters when you team it with the book on technique and your stitch dictionaries.

Type 4 Several books with brilliant, over-the-top "I-could-never" patterns in it. Wild intarsia, cables that make Celtic knots look simple, lace that drips complexity and makes your mind reel. Even if you're never going to knit the patterns, it is the stuff that knitterly inspiration comes from. Aim high. Dream big.

Type 5 A few books with stories about knitting, ideas about knitting, and tales of people living a knitting lifestyle. Although you may never fall down the rabbit hole and make every breathing second of your life from this moment forward about knitting, it's very normalizing and comforting to read about people who do.

THE RIGHT TOOL FOR THE JOB

My uncle Tupper is a carpenter. He's been a carpenter most of his life, and he has many, many tools. The last time I visited him I went into his garage and noted (with some surprise) that he had 14 kinds of saws. This shocked me. How many ways could you need to cut up stuff? My uncle started to explain them then, probably because a lot of what I'm thinking comes straight out of my mouth. This one was a circular saw, and it cuts big pieces of wood in a straight line. That one over there was a jigsaw, and it cuts scrolls and curves in wood. That one over there cuts laminates, and the big one with a table cuts sheets of plywood. He had a handsaw, a band saw, a compound miter saw, a trim saw — 14 saws, all necessary and useful. I left with a new attitude about all my knitting stuff.

Having the right tools matters, and all the knitting stuff I have isn't silly, useless, or even an odd obsession. While people are going to come into my house and let loose with a low whistle when they see my needle collection, I know my knitting patterns, books, row counters, and tape measures are the stuff of my occupation and inspiration, and having 17 stitch dictionaries and 54 circular needles in wood, metal, and plastic is no different from Uncle Tupper having 14 saws. Every scrap of pattern adds up to potential.

I really think the saws are more shocking.

four

GAUGE, SWATCHES,
and Learning
to Accept Them

ONCE UPON A TIME, somewhere in the world in a house full of wool, a knitter had an idea. She sat at a table with her needles and her paper and she knit up her idea, writing down her pattern as she made it up. When she was done, she measured how many stitches and rows she had gotten to the inch and wrote it down. This number she wrote down is the concept of gauge. Now, if you want to knit what she did, all you have to do is follow her pattern and match the unique tension that her knitting had, so even though you and this knitter have never met, and your knitting style will never be like hers, while you knit her pattern your work can be identical and (at least somewhat) predictable.

Simple, right?

WHY DOES GAUGE MATTER?

Gauge is discussed more than any other knitting idea and this is probably because it's the most important concept in knitting. Needles, yarn, patterns, technique . . . these are all ideas that relate to gauge, and very few things in knitting (except maybe, and only maybe, what color you knit with) don't relate back to gauge. It's also the thing that gives knitters the most grief.

If you go into a yarn shop full of knitters and ask them to tell you about gauge, two will tell you their current project is turning out huge even though they "got gauge," one will tell you her current project is turning out too small even though she "got gauge," the one by the window will say she "always gets gauge" (and everyone will glare at her), and one knitter will sob helplessly because she's cast on a new sweater six times, tried a gauge swatch nine times, changed needle sizes more often than most people change their minds, and, still the last time she measured a swatch she was only "close."

In Canada and the United Kingdom (and in patterns hailing from those countries), knitters often refer to the number of stitches to any given area as "tension" and knit "tension squares" instead of the "gauge swatches" you find in the United States. Despite the difference in terminology, knitters seem to get messed up over it at about the same rate, but the term *tension* does make for better jokes. Not too long ago, at a restaurant with a bunch of Canadian knitters, a waiter offered wine. One knitter declined, saying "No thank you, alcohol affects my tension," and another quipped back, "Me too, but my knitting stays the same."

PROS AND CONS

Because gauge is the most important concept in knitting, there are those who believe it's the root of all knitting trouble. These knitters, no matter what goes wrong with your knitting, will blame gauge. If it's too big, if it's too small, if the color runs, it's stolen by pirates and pecked half to death by a parrot before you can pull it away . . . when you take it to other knitters for sympathy and advice, one of them will say, "It's the gauge."

Someone, looking at the massive sleeves or the too tight neckline or the holes from the beak of a wild parrot and then fingering the stitches and noting the running dye or the misshapen shoulders, will — especially if there is no other explanation for the pit of despair and the nightmare that your knitting has become, even if you've just explained that the whole trouble with the sweater is coming from a stitch in the pattern that you don't understand, or you missed the directions for the sleeve cap — ignore all of this, look you in the eye, and say, "Did you get gauge? Maybe your gauge is off."

Then there are knitters on the other side of the coin. These are knitters who can't seem to accept that gauge really does matter and that you have to understand a little about it to get predictable results. These people are forever turning up at knitting circles with enormous hats, mittens for giants, and sweaters with necklines too small to go over a poodle's head. There they stand, morosely caressing their forlorn and disappointing knitting, complaining that nothing ever works out for them. These knitters, when you come up to them and say, "Oh dear, this is a classic gauge problem," will look at you and admit they didn't knit a swatch, don't ever knit a swatch, don't think swatch knitting is smart: in fact, their other hobby is mocking those who knit swatches and pointing and laughing at them behind their backs.

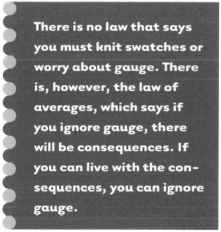

There is no law that says you must knit swatches or worry about gauge. There is, however, the law of averages, which says if you ignore gauge, there will be consequences. If you can live with the consequences, you can ignore gauge.

KNOWING WHEN TO RESPECT IT

Having been both of those knitters at some point in my life, I've come to believe that there's a time and a place for everything, and that there are times when a healthy

Gauge is not some magical thing. There is no incredible standard among designers and their test knitters. Each individual pattern has a gauge that is a reflection of the unique tension of the person who knit it up. Therefore, it is impossible to say "I always knit to gauge." How can you automatically hit the tension of this unknown knitter?

respect for gauge, like a healthy respect for fire and floods, is appropriate. Sweaters, for example. A difference of ¼ inch in a swatch could mean a difference of four inches in a finished sweater. Bad news, big mojo, and, worse, clearly significant in terms of potential knitting disaster.

On the other hand, ignoring the subtleties of gauge (or deciding to lie to your subconscious knitter) when you're working on a shawl is not nearly so problematic. A shawl that comes out a few inches (or feet) in an unexpected direction will still yield something you can wear. It might be an afghan, a scarf, or a kerchief instead of a shawl, but it's still going to be a knitted item of some usefulness.

You have to look at what your relative gauge risk (RGR) is and decide how just how seriously you're going to take gauge, swatching, and their attendant hysteria with each individual project.

If you're already a knitter, you know all about gauge. In the beginning, it's the bane of your existence, and as you get more experienced it becomes a tool you can use to fine-tune your knitting. Like a sculptor, you give a little, you take a little, you tweak here and there. Is the pattern a bit too big? Too small? Does it lack drape? Does it flare at the bottom? Gauge, my friends, gauge is the answer to all of this.

FIVE TIMES YOU DON'T NEED TO GET GAUGE

On the following page, you'll find the 10 times when you need to pay attention to gauge. I tried hard to come up with 10 times that you could ignore gauge but it turns out that there are only five that I could think of. I tried to get you off the hook, I really did. I phoned friends, I sat in on knitting groups, I searched the Web. But, it turns out there really are twice as many times when you have to pay attention than there are when you can ignore it. I'm sorry.

Scenario 1   **If you're knitting a dishcloth.** Think about it. What would you knit to test gauge? A square? That's a dishcloth.

Scenario 2   **If you're a "process" knitter** and the thought of ripping back your work as many times as it takes is really no problem for you, as it's all knitting and, darn it, that's what you like.

Scenario 3   **If you're making something for which size doesn't matter** (a scarf or a shawl, for example).

Scenario 4   **If you have tons of yarn.** Buckets. So much that if your gauge is way off and you end up needing 17 more skeins to finish, you don't care. (We won't discuss who's going to fit into something that takes 17 extra skeins: you're the one who's going to have a sweater that's a house cozy.)

Scenario 5   **If you're knitting something that starts with a few stitches** and increases as you go. If something is getting bigger slowly, you can stop when it's big enough. A truly brilliant example of this is a hat knit from the "top down."

10 TIMES

Ten Times When You Should Worry About Gauge

1. If you want your work to be exactly the same (or as close as possible, considering that you changed the neckline, the yarn, and the cable pattern) as the sweater in the picture on your pattern.

2. If your bust is 36 inches and you'd like the sweater to be related to that fact in any kind of way.

3. If you're worried about your yarn supply. Different gauges take different amounts of yarn. Even with a scarf for which the gauge element doesn't matter much, if you're knitting to a much larger gauge, you may run out of yarn. (I'd tell you how I learned this, but it was so painful that I still can't speak of it.)

4. If you're up against a deadline and you don't have much time. Pulling back a hat and trying again because you took a chance is no big deal unless it's Christmas Eve, the hat is your dad's present, and he doesn't have a head the size of an all-you-can-eat salad bowl.

5 If you're the sort of knitter who hates ripping out whole projects and finds it emotionally demoralizing.

6 If you're knitting a yarn like mohair, chenille, or anything else that doesn't hold up well (or is snatched bald) when it's ripped out and started over 26 times during the process of trial and error.

7 If you didn't swatch for your last sweater and it worked out really, really well. (The knitting goddess can seldom resist an opportunity to smack you down.)

8 If you're absolutely convinced you don't need to swatch because you "always get gauge." (See number 7.)

9 If you don't have many friends or if your friends are all the same size. If you have an assortment of friends and family in various shapes and sizes, you can just give away the wrong-size knitted thing to someone it fits.

10 If you made the first mitten of a pair six months ago when you were a new knitter and you're only now knitting the second one. Things (like your tension, your emotional state, and your relative skill) change and your gauge changes with them.

SWATCHES AND THE GAME YOU PLAY WITH THEM

There is a certain truth to swatches, and it's an unfortunate one. It turns out that the bigger the swatch, the greater the chance of accuracy. This means, naturally, that the best gauge swatches are the projects themselves, but we've already determined that you're probably attempting to get out of knitting the project several times.

HOW TO DO IT

Whatever you decide, don't skimp on the swatch. As much as I try to get you out of it, you should knit a gauge swatch (or a tension square, depending on your country of origin) that's big enough that you can measure 4 inches (or 10 centimeters) across to get your stitch gauge and the same amount up and down to get your row gauge. Cast on (using the cast-on that the pattern calls for, if it

If you hate to knit swatches, are eager to get going, and just read what I said about the best swatches being the projects themselves, take a good look at your intentions and ask yourself, "Is there any part of this sweater that would make a good swatch?" Could you begin the sleeve? Many sleeves start small enough that you wouldn't mind ripping back one when if wasn't right. How about a pocket, a pillow, or the front of a cardigan? If no part of the project leaps out as the perfect guinea pig, then how about knitting a matching accessory? (Obviously, if you're knitting an accessory, you know I think you should just dive in.)

tells you) at least as many stitches as you think it'll take to cover 4 inches (or 10 cm), plus at least an inch more for insurance, and then knit along in the stitch your pattern calls for. I can't stress enough the importance of doing this. If your pattern calls for stockinette, this is what you knit the swatch in. If it's garter stitch, then do that. If it's cables and lace (may the knitting goddess bless you), do the lace and cables.

Many knitters have different tension on circulars and straights. So, it's important to work the gauge square with the needle type that you're going to use later. This is especially important for a mixed-needle project. I was making one where the body was knit on circular needles and the sleeves were knit on straights, and I learned the hard way (don't I always) that my gauge is different with the two kinds of needle. A smarter knitter than I am would have knit a gauge swatch with the circulars and a swatch with the straights, and tried to match the gauge in both. It would have been nice to discover this quirk of my knitting style sometime before I sewed in the sleeves and discovered they were large enough to hold a litter of kittens.

If your project is knit circularly, you can knit a circular swatch without casting on enough to go all the way around a circular needle. Cast on the swatch stitches, knit them (or purl them, or whatever your pattern dictates), and then, without turning, slide back your work to the beginning, reach the yarn across the back loosely, and start at the right-hand side again. Repeat this until you have a good-sized swatch.

When you've knit a few inches (at least two or three) cast off (if you're a good knitter) or simply take the knitting off the needles (if you're lazy and your yarn is not the unraveling kind). It is important both to knit a few inches and to take the knitting off the needles to measure gauge. Both the cast-on edge and the needle can distort your stitches as much as several shots of vodka, so your aim is to knit enough that you can measure a stretch of knitting that's uninfluenced by the edge and the needle.

When you have a sample chunk of knitting knit in the style and manner of your project-to-be, you're ready for the next phase of swatch management: washing. When the swatch is finished, treat it exactly as you'll treat the finished item. If it's for a lace shawl, wash and block it, and if it's for a sweater, wash, pat it into shape the way you will the sweater, and leave it to dry.

This step is the one most often missed by those swatch knitters who go on to unhappy endings. Surprising things can happen to yarn when it hits water, and the astute and cautious knitter washes her swatch exactly the way that the garment or item will be washed when the project is done. You can make it dry faster by putting a fan nearby to blow on it.

When the swatch is dry, unpin it (if it was pinned down) and find one of those elusive tape measures and

A gauge square is a misnomer. There's no reason you can't do gauge triangles or stars if you want (and now that I think of it, gauge stars could make pretty cool Christmas decorations). Imagine coming up to Christmas season and having a swatch from every project you'd knit all year to tie on to packages or hang on the tree. Sure, your family would think the knitting thing had gone way too far, and maybe they'd call the cookie truck to take you away for a little "rest," but . . . doesn't a little rest sound good?

some pins. You are now ready to attack *stitch gauge*. Starting at least ½ inch in from an edge, insert a pin to mark your starting place. Then measure 4 inches (or 10 cm) from that spot and mark the ending point with a pin. Now, count, with all the honesty you can muster, how many stitches are between the two marks. Then do it again. Then give the swatch a shake, and do it again. The number of stitches between your markers is the stitch gauge.

Check the pattern with some care. Somewhere on it will be a bit about tension or gauge. Read this part to make sure you aren't making assumptions. Nine knitting patterns out of 10 will have you measure gauge over 4 inches (or 10 cm) Then, out of the blue, you come across a pattern that calls for something else. Take a minute to register that the pattern writer wants 20 stitches to 4 inches, and not 20 stitches to 2 inches. Not catching this can make you think unkind thoughts about yourself and others.

If you're lucky, your gauge will match the pattern's. If you're unlucky, it won't and you'll have to try again.

If you have FEWER stitches to the inch than the pattern calls for, you need to make the stitches SMALLER so more will fit in the same space. Use a SMALLER needle.

If you have MORE stitches to the inch than the pattern calls for, you need to make the stitches BIGGER so fewer will fill the same space. Use a BIGGER needle.

I'd feel guilty about telling you something so obvious, but when it's late at night, it's your third swatch, nothing is working, and you're fraying at the edges, it can be really helpful to have the rule written down in black and white. In the heat of gauge battle, things are forgotten.

Now take the measuring tape and deal with row gauge. *Row gauge* is how many rows of knitting (measured up and down) fit in the prescribed area, and it's also the bane of many a knitter's existence. Knitters are forever getting stitch gauge only to realize they don't have row gauge, knitting a new swatch that gets row gauge but not stitch gauge —only to want to run themselves through with a knitting needle because they think they'll never get both. It's a problem.

Given a choice between getting stitch gauge and getting row gauge, take stitch gauge every time. Row gauge is easier to compensate for; just add a few rows or decrease a few. You should still try to get gauge on both; I'm just saying that if you must choose, you'll be less likely to want to feed your own ears to a wild boar if you settle for stitch gauge.

MORE THAN MEASURING

A swatch is not just about gauge, and it's not the only reason to knit one. (Although you have to admit that gauge disasters being so frequent, gauge alone is a pretty good reason.) Knitting a swatch is also like a first date between knitter and yarn. You get to know each other, you converse, you see how the yarn behaves when you handle it, you discover if it's soft or harsh, you decide whether the pattern you've picked is right for this individual yarn. You begin to get a sense of the potential your relationship holds: is it a keeper? Or are you going to have to dump it faster than a 42-year-old man with an action-figure collection and his mommy on speed-dial.

FOUR THINGS TO DO WITH ALL YOUR SWATCHES

1. Put them in a knitter's journal with project notes underneath.
2. Use them as coasters. (Work with me.)
3. Save them up to make a blanket of all the different squares sewn together.
4. Keep them in a box in the closet, intending to sew them up, but don't. Every time you clean the closet, take them out, feel guilty that you haven't done it yet, and put them back in. Repeat for 20 years, then — maybe — throw them away.

DENIAL AIN'T JUST A RIVER IN EGYPT
(A Cautionary Tale for Knitters)

My friend Emma recently knit a sweater, or, to be precise, my friend Emma recently intended to knit a sweater. She took her hand-spun and an appropriate pattern and launched. Now, Emma is what I would call a typical knitter with a side of independence. She's conscientious when it comes to her knitting: She knows and understands the ways of the swatch and respects the mojo of the swatch. I've watched her swatch. Emma understands, as most thoughtful knitters do, that even though swatches are an imperfect system, they're all we have.

Emma knew all of this, and even though she wanted a sweater that would fit, she maintained she didn't mind being messed over if gauge didn't work out quite right. She was feeling flexible. If she had to rip back, so be it. No problem. Like millions of knitters before her, Emma understood that in simply beginning a sweater, even though thousands of patterns had warned her not to, even though millions of knitters have suffered before her, even though the first page of every knitting book is about knitting a swatch, she was turning her back on gauge, predictability, and the mysteries of tension, and instead accepting consequences, hours of possible reknitting, and yet another funny-looking addition to the wardrobe of sweaters that are in the "sack" family of styling.

There come times in every story where you realize that things could have changed, a place where the plot could have turned right or left, toward darkness or light, bringing on disaster or insight. Writers call these places in a plot "turning points," and beginning a sweater without any regard for tension is one of them. Emma began to knit her cardigan, casting on for the neck and working downward, increasing as the pattern directed. She did become aware that the sweater was perhaps going to have a little more ease than she intended. *Note:* This was the first turning point. Despite the way the sweater was running toward the big side of things, Emma didn't measure anything, so she could perhaps stop increasing and make the sweater a little smaller. No, no . . . Emma kept going. She turned toward the darkness, the snare that gauge had set for her.

Emma kept knitting, and as she knit, the sweater spread across her lap like a lava flow. The thing was looking big. Still, eternally hopeful (ever reluctant to rip out the monstrosity at yet another turning point), Emma kept it scrunched up on her circular needle and bravely went on knitting.

Circular needles can be particularly deceptive, as the whole work stays curled up in an innocent-looking circle. If you have suspicions, use a darning needle and thread the live stitches onto a length of yarn so you can have an honest look at it. Naturally, this will destroy any illusions you have, but as painful as that sounds, it could help. If you're really emotionally invested, try a glass of wine beforehand. It doesn't fix gauge problems, but who cares?

Emma kept knitting, putting aside some stitches for the armholes, where she would later pick up stitches for the arms and knit them on. She kept knitting but she started revising her plan a little. Because the sweater was obviously a little "roomy," she decided she wasn't actually knitting a cardigan sweater — it was now a jacket. Yeah, that's it. A jacket. A big, bulky jacket. Emma bought a zipper.

Emma kept knitting, even though she was starting to wonder why she seemed to be running out of yarn. She absolutely had enough yarn to knit herself a sweater when she began, so where was it all going? At the rate this jacket (note that Emma has assimilated the new project goal seamlessly, allowing her to believe that this thing is still the right size) was going it wasn't going to get two sleeves. She began to wonder whether there was such a thing as a short-sleeved bulky-wool jacket.

Emma kept knitting and eventually came to cast off the largish jacket, and here's where the story gets incredible. She cast off the body of the jacket, saw that it was big, knew the gauge was off, knew it was too big . . . and then sewed in the zipper.

It was astounding. It was like she had so much invested in it that she couldn't see the enormousness of the sweater in front of her. When people saw it, they asked her odd things, like "Isn't that sweater too short?" (It's formidable width played a trick on the eyes. To appear proportionately long enough for its width, it would have had to be almost five feet long.) My favorite, often whispered behind her back, was "Are you out of your mind?"

Emma kept knitting. This impressed the heck out of me; you really have to be deluded or demented to miss the fact that you've knit something as big as this jacket. It also impressed me that she could sink this deeply into denial. It's boggling that she looked that monstrous sweater in the eye and then picked up and knit the

Knitting things that gradually increase in size instead of decrease in size is one way to know you're in the uncertain world of gauge. If you're increasing and things are bigger than expected, stop increasing sooner and perhaps you'll save your item. If things are smaller than expected, increase for longer and maybe you'll still have something you can wear. If, however, you cast on and decrease, nothing short of "the big rip" will save you if the thing is too big or too small. It's something to consider if you're going to dabble in the dark art of swatchless gauge.

sleeves, but that's exactly what she did. She knit and knit, and we were all appalled. We thought about an intervention. We wondered whether she would wear it when it was done. We wondered if we should take her aside and say, gently, "Emma, it's not going to work. You have had a gauge accident. You need to step away from the knitting." We didn't, though. We let her keep going. Even now I don't know why we didn't intercede. I think it was like she was sleepwalking and we didn't know if it would hurt her to wake her. My husband says that's what we tell ourselves so we don't have to own up to being horrible people who thought it was really, really funny.

Emma kept knitting, and we all waited to see what would happen. Would it hit her all at once? Would she cry when finally she saw it with her own two eyes? When was she going to see what we could see? Maybe when she tried it on and realized she could be leaping from a plane with only this parachute of a sweater to save her . . .

Mistakes with gauge are painful and difficult to accept. This is largely because there is absolutely no one else you can blame. Nobody. It's not the designer's fault, it's not the yarn's fault, the editor didn't miss an error, it's not "just one of those things." It's not because your mate annoyed you while you were knitting and messed with your concentration. You can't blame it on an unhappy childhood or an inability to cope with a fear of emotional commitment. There is no-one to blame but you — and this happened because you didn't spend a wee bit of time knitting a tiny square.

In the end (as Emma kept knitting), it was the sweater that stopped her. Finally, unable to see the truth, blinded by her love for wool and her faith that anything knitted was good, finally, Emma ran out of yarn mid-sleeve.

This story ends here only because Emma was knitting with hand-spun. For reasons I can't fully explain, reasons to do with pain and knitting and hope, if it had been a yarn that she could have gotten more of, she would have kept going. I know this because when Emma brought the sweater to our knitting night for us to help her rip it back for a do-over, she explained (as she lay what looked like a brown, woolen, hand-knit, five-room, cabled refugee tent on the table) that the sweater was "not fitting." We were stunned by her language. Not fitting? This sweater was "not fitting" exactly the way apples are not motorcycles. Not fitting? It was time to wake her from the dream, and quickly, before she cast on again. Thinking fast, we did the only thing we could. We asked her to try it on, and then swiftly — before she could get the shameful thing off her — we zipped a whole other full-size knitter inside with her.

It was cruel, but gauge is a vicious mistress, and all is fair in love and war.

Altering your plan is the first sign not only that you're not knitting what you thought you were, but also that you may not know what you're knitting at all. This, combined with a nagging sense of doom that you have to ignore, is a sign that the knitter may be experiencing a gauge problem of some significance.

REVERTING TO TYPE

You know, sometimes I just jump in. I don't swatch, I just start, and there are times when this is appropriate, or at least I delude myself into thinking it's appropriate. Really, I tell myself, I have a shot at getting gauge right enough that it's worth saving the time. Yes, it's possible that you or I will nail gauge right out of the gate. I like to think that there's just as much of a chance as not that I'll have gauge the first time I cast on for a project. This delusion is what lets me put 299 stitches for a shawl on the needles without knitting a swatch — because this time I'm convinced (no matter how many times I've had to rip out things in the past) that things will be different. That this time, I'll get lucky. Sometimes that actually happens.

Really, though, when you think about it, there's very little chance that you or I will get it right without a few attempts. (Think of this as you swatch and swatch and feel stupid for not being able to nail it.) There are, all things considered, and with the world being as bright and varied as it is, many ways to get it wrong, and only one way to get it right. Statistically speaking, your chances are not good.

This used to bug the wool off me. I want to start now. I don't want to knit a swatch. I don't want to wait while I wash and dry it, I don't want to delay while I hunt up a tape measure. That's me: Even instant gratification takes too long.

One time while I was knitting a swatch and complaining about it, my husband said, "Nobody's forcing you to do it, honey," and I stopped and had a (rare) moment of clarity. He had a point. I choose to knit and I love it, even though some parts of it do make me want to rasp off my eyebrows with a nail file, and it's my choice to pursue it. I could do something else, something with no swatches, something like collecting spoons or vacuuming. Instead, I persist — the rewards are great.

Sometimes when I'm knitting I watch my hands very carefully. I highly recommend this. I've been knitting for a lot of years and I've made probably millions of stitches, but I can still be taken by surprise when I just sit and watch my hands. I'm astonished that they know how to

Knitting Rules!

do this. That they can just knit along, making tiny little movements that are automatic and interesting. I watch the pointer finger on my left hand. If I were describing to someone "how to knit," I'm sure she'd give up instantly when I told her what that finger is to do. It holds the next stitch in line, then moves it into position, then briefly touches the front of the stitch while the right needle is inserted, then spaces the remaining stitches and moves the next into line. It's so complicated and graceful, and I didn't even know I was doing it. (It's usually at this point that my awe and astonishment are replaced by a total lack of comprehension that I can be capable of this beautiful knitter-finger dance and then still be such a klutz that I regularly fall *up* the stairs, spill coffee, and break a glass a week, but I digress.) As I watch my hands do what they do, I realize that this is about gauge too, that this is why I have a different gauge from the knitter who knit the pattern or the knitter who thought it up, or the other knitters who have done this pattern. I am a unique knitter. Nobody does this exactly the way that I do, or exactly the way anybody else does, and that's the beauty of gauge. It makes us match someone we've never met who has a whole finger dance of her own that we've never even seen. Pretty cool.

Now I try to be a little more Zen about swatching and the math of knitting. It's an investment in my art, and, you know, knitting swatches is still knitting, and I like knitting.

The finger dance is the reason knitters will always revert to type. This means that if you're a very tight knitter and you decide to knit more loosely to correct your gauge, chances are you'll knit a sweater that begins loose (while you're focusing) and gets tighter as you relax back into your own, unique style. Better to go up a needle size than to try to change your style. Nobody knits the way you do, and that's worth embracing.

Gauge Swatches

8 THINGS

Eight Things to Know About Swatches

1 Swatches lie. There is no getting around this. You can knit a swatch and still have a gauge problem. This is partly because big pieces of knitting (like your sweater) behave differently from small pieces of knitting (like your swatch). It's also because when you knit stuff, the law of gravity comes into play. Once you get a sweater knit and hanging on a person, gravity begins to pull on it and you can get some pretty significant gauge surprises. There are also laws of knitting that become a factor. The one I believe is involved with gauge is called the Element of Surprise. The way swatches lie is simply another one of knitting's little jokes designed to keep things interesting.

2 The bigger the better. Sometimes the things going on with gauge are subtle. (I'd say "naked to the human eye" but that sounds bitter.) The bigger your swatch, the more obvious the trouble. There's no magic size that reveals all flaws (except "actual size"), but I think you should aim to do more than just a couple of rows. Did I mention the lying? Don't cheat. No squashing, mushing, or stretching a swatch to make it work. Measure it exactly the way it is and suck it up if it's wrong. Ignoring a half stitch you don't want to believe is there is almost as bad as the swatch lying, and the consequences are the same.

3. Always wash a swatch. Some pretty funky things can happen to yarns when they hit water, and you don't want surprises when those funky things happen to a sweater that took away 60 hours of your life. Wash a swatch the way you'll wash the finished item.

4. Don't expect a swatch to be an absolute. I can't over-emphasize the possibility that you'll do everything right and you'll still have a gauge problem. The only perfectly accurate gauge swatch is one knit to scale.

5. Gauge isn't used just to match the tension of the pattern. It's also a way to affect the way your knitting looks and feels. Are you knitting a scarf and it feels too stiff? Go up a needle size or two and give it more drape. Use gauge to fine-tune your knitting.

6. Even if you "get gauge" when you substitute yarns, there may be other changes. Using a yarn of a texture or fiber different from the original can make things very, very different from what you planned. Gauge isn't the only thing that matters. Use your instincts.

7. You're going to meet knitters who tell you row gauge doesn't matter and that they ignore it. They may be right. They may be wrong. Until I can figure that out for myself, though, I'm going to pay a little attention.

8. Swatches lie. (It bears repeating.)

five

HATS

HATS ARE A WONDER and a gift and the best thing you could ever choose to knit. I know I'm making a firm statement there, but I can say it quite honestly because I'm not knitting one right now and I have the clarity of distance. I understand you may not feel the same love for hats that I do if you have one glaring at you from your knitting basket; if that's the case, perhaps you'll see my point if you come back to this chapter sometime when your arse is being kicked by a shawl instead.

Despite all the good reasons for knitting hats (see pages 104–5 for just a few), as a knitter you're going to meet the occasional person who hates hats. Maybe, just to add insult to injury, the person actually hates just knitted hats. What do you do? What does a dedicated, loving, talented, and committed hat-knitting knitter do when faced with that kind of personal attack? Knit mittens. Hats aren't worth a missionary effort, and studies show (I asked around) that if you knit for a hat resister, nine times out of 10 the hat ends up at Goodwill or stuffed down the back of his closet. One out of 10 times the recipient keeps the hat around (reluctantly and wears it when he sees you). This is not good for a relationship. Walk away; knit where you're appreciated. Other people love hats.

Of course, there are also those with an overwhelming fear of hat head. Hat head is a sad affliction wherein the chosen hat and the selected hairstyle are grossly incompatible. The unfortunate combination results in a condition that can be hidden only with the application of another hat. It's a vicious cycle, and one you need to know, as victims will both abhor hats and hold them in the highest regard.

10 REASONS

Ten Reasons to Knit Hats

1 Your mother was right. (Again.) Thirty to 50 percent of our body heat is lost through the head. This means that for much less knitting, yarn, and time, hats are at least as warm as sweaters. This is good news for knitters who, like me, live in Canada and have a short attention span.

2 Hats appear to be excluded from the normal rules and restrictions that picky people make up about their wardrobes. A man or woman who won't wear colors or stripes or anything that falls outside of an extremely personal and inflexible set of guidelines will often own a hat that breaks all of these rules.

3 Hats are, as far as knitting goes, pretty small. When I need the thrill of a knitting victory and I want it quickly, a hat gives a fast payoff. Sometimes I'll knit a hat during a sweater project just to take the edge off.

4 Hats are comparatively easy. I won't say they're easy, because if I do, someone who's out there having a bad time with a Fair Isle beret knit at 30 stitches to the inch is going to write me a very nasty letter, but compared to a sweater or socks (especially those that are Fair Isle and 30 stitches to the inch), a hat is a walk in the park.

Knitting Rules!

5. Human head sizes are hugely variable. The diameter of a preemie's head can be as little as 9 inches, whereas a linebacker's could be as great as 27 inches. That's quite a range. Knit on: it will fit somebody you know.

6. Hats take very little yarn. They're good for leftovers, for one skein you adore, or for trying out a little bit of yarn to figure out if you want to invest in enough for a bigger project. If you discover, for example, that the brand-new merino you've been coveting for six months pills so much that it should be in rehab, it's a lot easier to take if you have a hat rather than a sleeve.

7. Hats are needed in all seasons. In the summertime, you can knit lacy cotton caps or baby sun hats; in the spring, bonnets; and in the fall, jaunty berets. In winter, you can switch to hard-core hats with earflaps. See? Hats are year-round projects. Try that with mittens, and you're going to look so stupid in July.

8. There are as many ways to make a hat as there are knitters. A hat can be knit in the flat, in the round, and on straights, circulars, or DPNs. You can use super-chunky wool or delicate silk. No matter how you like to knit, I promise there's a hat pattern out there for you.

9. Hats get lost. So do mittens, but at least you can put mittens on a string. Although most knitters see hat loss as a problem, I see it as an advantage. This constant hat turnover means the odds are extremely good that someone you know will need another hat soon.

10. Hats are singular. Unlike mittens, socks, and the accursed perpetual sleeves, hats have only one part: no sides, no front, no back, no mate to slog through after the thrill is gone. Hats come in joyous, simple, forever "ones."

WHAT HATS HAVE OVER SCARVES

A hat can be the simplest of knitting affairs and I think an international campaign to install a hat instead of a scarf as the first project for a knitter should be undertaken immediately.

Why? you ask (I can hear you from here). Why? For starters, a hat is much less of a major to-do than a scarf. Sure, scarves are practical, and no, I don't mean for you to give up on knitting them, but a scarf takes stamina. Just think about how it goes. You learn to cast on, you learn to knit (or purl) and get practice, but then it starts. A scarf goes on for entirely too long once you've mastered the basics. You get good at back-and-forth knitting and then it's just 47 miles of straight knitting until you get to add a third skill: casting off. Unless you're a knitter who doesn't mind boredom, you're really going to need to add "persistence" as a fourth skill.

A hat is a perfect place to experiment. If you choose a simple pattern, there is absolutely no reason not to try making some serious design changes. Ask yourself "What would happen if I . . ." and then try it. No one has ever suffered a lightning strike as punishment for knitting a bad hat. If it's hideous when you're done, be delighted you learned your lesson on a hat instead of on a sweater and bury the thing in the backyard.

A hat stands in sharp contrast to a scarf as the perfect teaching tool. The only thing that scarves have over hats is that a crappy first scarf can be tucked into a coat — a crappy first hat is out in public.

Knitting Rules!

Scarf Rescue Hat

A while ago, I discovered a way to get out of finishing a scarf and I wrote it down so anyone else who has started a scarf and has awakened to the reality that she can't take the heat of another 40 garter stitches can move on. I suppose you could just haul off and finish the thing, but I have to tell you that I think you'll enjoy it more when you bend a scarf to your will.

Ingredients

You'll need some yarn — the type is up to you, as this hat works with just about everything. You'll also need needles of an appropriate size to knit your yarn into a fabric you like. (It's good for it to be not too floppy; floppy hats don't flatter many people. Naturally, if you're the exception to this rule and pretty much look good only in floppy hats, you can blow off that suggestion.)

How to Do It

1. **Knit a swatch.** (You knew I was going to say that, didn't you?) Begin by casting on about as many stitches as it takes to cover your hand, from the base of the palm to the tip of your longest finger plus 2 inches. This is a fairly big swatch, but if you're lucky, it'll be your hat.

2. **Knit back and forth for a while.** Garter stitch is good (plain knitting every row), until you have 2 to 3 inches.

3. **Now measure the width of the swatch.** If you're lucky, it'll still measure about the length of your hand plus 2 inches and you can proceed directly to step 6. If it measures much bigger, you're still okay, because you can just fold up the extra and your hat will have a brim.

If, after starting to knit, you decide to change a scarf into a hat, the scarf needs to be at least as wide as your hand is tall (from the bottom of the palm to the tip of your longest finger) plus about 2 inches.

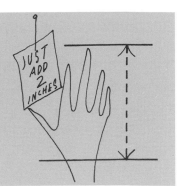

4 **If the width of the swatch is smaller than the hand height plus 2 inches, you'll have to make an adjustment.** First, count the number of stitches in 1 inch and write down this number. For the purpose of making this simple, let's imagine you find that there are 5 stitches in each inch. Now go back to the hand-height-plus-2 measurement. Let's say your hand is 8 inches, so 8 + 2 = 10. Now multiply (don't panic — this is the only math in this hat) the number of stitches to the inch by the hand-measurement number. **For my hat, this is:**
5 (stitches to the inch) × 10 (the length of my hand plus 2 inches) = 50 (the magic number)

5 **From here it's a breeze.** Cast on the magic number of stitches and start knitting.

6 **Knit until the fabric is long enough to go around your head.** If it's not for your head, measure the circumference of the recipient's head. If you're trying to be discreet (and there really is no discreet way to measure someone's head), check out How Big is Your Head? (at right) to make an educated guess.

7 **Bind off.**

8 **Sew together the beginning and ending edges to form a tube of sorts, kind of like a very wide headband.** This seam marks the center back of the hat.

9 **Thread a piece of yarn and run the needle through the top row of stitches along one edge, then gather them up to make a traditional-looking cap.** Pull the thread tight and fasten off. Celebrate not just a good-looking hat, but that you didn't have to knit 57 life-draining inches on a scarf. (Not that I don't like scarves; they have their place. As a matter of fact, see chapter 7.)

Once you've finished your hat and you love it, take a good look. I held mine in my hands and not only did I feel great about not having to finish a scarf that I was really not enamored of, but I also saw the world of possibility loom before me.

HOW BIG IS YOUR HEAD?

Head sizes are extremely variable. Hats don't have to fit exactly, as knitting tends to be stretchy, but it's better for a hat to be a little big than too small. A big hat still goes

Typical Head Sizes

Age	Head Circumference (approximate)
Preemie	12"/30 cm
Small newborn	13"/33 cm
Large newborn	14"/36 cm
1 year	17"/43 cm
2–5 years	18"/45 cm
5–10 years	19"/48 cm
Small adult	20"/50 cm
Large adult	24"/60 cm

In a hat-knitting emergency (don't smirk — you know you've had one) when you have no measuring tape, no chart, and no clue, remember this: Roughly speaking, in humans older than six years, a person's head circumference is about three times the width of his or her outstretched hand, measured thumb to pinkie.

on, but a small hat . . . well, it's better for it to be too big. Babies grow quickly, some knitters knit slowly. You might want to factor that in when you choose a size. There is little more infuriating to a knitter than having someone outgrow something while it's on the needles.

There are going to be exceptions. My husband has a 66-cm (26 inch) head, and near as I can tell, although that's pretty big-headed according to the chart, he seems fairly normal. (A little odd, yes, but he doesn't look funny or anything.)

An advantage of this variety of human head sizes is that if you manage to knit something between 12 and 27 inches (30 and 70 cm), you'll find someone it'll fit. Cultivate a wide circle of friends.

VARIATIONS ON FINISHING THE TOP

Sew together the top edges in a straight line and wear the hat with the points front and back. Try it. It has a romantic, *Dr. Zhivago*, Russian-winter sort of feel, especially if you knit it wide enough to have a fold-up brim and you rename yourself Lara.

Sew it flat and attach tassels to each point so you can wear the points side to side. (Admittedly, except for those rare "playful" days, this is a look that wears better on a six-year-old than on a 40-year-old CEO, but you be the judge.)

TEN VARIATIONS ON THE SCARF RESCUE HAT

Variation 1

Knit it in other yarns. Because this hat has such a flexible pattern, there's no reason you can't change the gauge every time you make one. A hat knit out of super-chunky yarn is going to look way different from one out of fingering weight, even if you knit them in the same manner.

Variation 2

Try it in other stitches. Keep in mind that this hat has no ribbing. This means that the one I made in stockinette stitch rolled faster than a hippie at Woodstock. Hats that are knit "around" need flat stitches so they will lie flat on your forehead. Seed stitch, moss stitch, basket weave, and patterns with a mix of knit and purl all work.

It's the combination of knit and purl stitches that makes knitting lie flat. If something you're knitting won't lie down, use a stitch that gives balance. Ribbing, moss, seed, and garter are all balanced and combine the yin and yang of knitting. (You could also try blocking the living daylights out of it, but, frankly, I don't think that will work.)

Variation 3

How about cables or Fair Isle? This hat has no decreases to botch your math. If you keep the first few stitches on the brim side in your non-rolling-stitch choice, the rest of the hat can be Fair Isle or cables. Think of the possibilities. (All I can think of is a penguin hat, but that's me.)

Variation 4

Lace. Same rules as for Fair Isle, but other than keeping that brim-edge solid, you could get really funky with it. Remember, of course, that lace has holes and is therefore not the warmest choice for a hat, but it would still be neat provided you aren't equipping an Arctic expedition.

Variation 5
Add stuff. Incorporate embroiderery on the hat; sew on buttons; get wild with tassels. What would you do to the hat if you could do anything? (*Hint*: You *can* do anything.)

WHO WEARS WHAT: HAT RULES

Before you launch a hat-knitting extravaganza, bolstered by the glowing things I've said about them, consider the following caveats.

Rule 1
Babies will wear hats — briefly. Mostly, a baby uses a hat to teach Mum and Dad a rollicking game of fetch.

Rule 2
Older children will only wear hats if they are a) cheap or b) ugly. The chances that your child will wear a hat you knit for him decreases exponentially with the class of wool and the seriousness of the effort required to knit it. For example: If you spend 50 hours knitting a hat with a Fair Isle band of frolicking monkeys (your child's favorite animal) and you special-ordered the perfect blue from Germany so that it could be in your little sweetie's favorite colors *and* it cost $45 to get it, your child, and I really can't stress this enough . . . Your child is not going to wear that hat. If, however, your crazy aunt Mabel dug around in her basement and came up with some plastic yarn from 1972 and spent 10 minutes knitting the ugliest, most unflattering hat you've ever seen — I mean, so ugly that it has superpowers — and then your aunt Mabel gives it to your kid and you think to yourself (feeling a

little shame), "Well, the joke's on you Aunt Mabel; Billy stuffs hand-knit hats behind the hamster cage," then Billy is going to wear that hat every day until he outgrows it and then cry for more.

Rule 3 **Teenagers do not wear hats** except in summer, while skateboarding, or as a fashion statement designed to humiliate or annoy you. Perfect example: a lovely 14-year-old girl who insists that if she doesn't wear a black skullcap with flames on it along with a powder blue party dress to your great-aunt Mavis's formal dinner party, then she will *die*. Remember the threat of frostbite means nothing to a teenager. He'll laugh at frostbite. He'll laugh at you. (Put the hat in the backpack. At −40 degrees, he'll put it on as long as there's no chance that you'll see him. Never speak of this.)

Rule 4 **Most men** will wear a fairly wide assortment of hats. I find this somewhat surprising, as these same men are inflexible in all other aspects of their wardrobe. It's a happy little quirk that men who look at you like you're trying to get them killed if you suggest a nice green shirt will become attached to odd, distinctive, or unusual hats. This tendency has not been sufficiently studied by anthropologists.

Rule 5 **Women are difficult.** A hat must be a flattering shape, the perfect colors, and not violate the hairstyle underneath. Women are very, very picky about hats. If I'm thinking about striking out and making a woman a hat, we have a long talk about the realities of my hat-knitting first.

The No-Pattern Hat

hat 2
RECIPE

One of the best things about hats (and there are many) is the way that one can be knit, spur of the moment, with no pattern and very little planning. If you have yarn and the needles that go with it, you can have a hat.

Ingredients

- **Yarn** (your choice)
- **Needles** that, when used with your yarn, give you a fabric you like (Use straight or circular, but if you choose to knit in the round you'll need a set of more or less matching double-pointed needles to finish the top of the hat when the stitches won't fit around the circular anymore.)
- **A darning needle** for sewing up
- **A measuring tape,** if you can find one (where do they go?)

How to Do It

1. You know what I'm going to say. **Knit a swatch** and find out how many stitches to the inch you're getting with the yarn and needles you have chosen.
2. **Measure around the head** of the recipient, or use the chart Typical Head Sizes (see page 110) to make an educated guess.
3. **Multiply the number of inches** around the head by the number of stitches to the inch. For example: If the intended head is 20 inches and you're getting 5 stitches to the inch, then 20 × 5 = 100 stitches to start with.

> **Number of stitches per inch × number of inches around head = number of stitches to cast on.**

4 **Cast on** the calculated number if you're knitting in the round or the calculated number plus two stitches (for the seams) if you're going back and forth.

5 **Knit** either around and around or back and forth (or do ribbing, or whatever turns your little crank) until the hat is long enough to reach the crown of the head (see Head Rules and Exceptions on page 118).

6 **When you reach the crown,** you have three choices. Which one you opt for has a lot to do with your personality and how close it is to the deadline for the hat.

- **Quick and dirty/Christmas Eve solution:** Do nothing. Knit to the top of the head, work an extra inch, then thread the yarn through the working stitches and gather them up tight. Sew the seam (if you have knit flat) and admire the finished hat in a self-congratulatory fashion. This makes a hat with a fetching gathered top and works best if you've used yarn that isn't too bulky, although if I'm really anxious to finish a hat, I can rationalize it any way I need to.

- **A little more time and effort:** For the next round (or row), knit two stitches together every three or four stitches. Work one row plain, then work one row with a decrease every other stitch. Work another row plain, and on the last row (or round . . . you know what I mean), knit two stitches together all the way across. Gather up the remaining stitches (triumphantly), and you're done.

> When in doubt, knit longer. A hat that's too long can be folded up, but a hat that's too short will be annoyingly tugged on for years to come.

- **Type A solution:** Count your stitches. Choose a number between 5 and 10 that divides into your total. For example, if you have 80 stitches in your hat, 8 is a good choice. Now work a row decreasing in groups of eight (or whatever your number is): Knit six; knit two together. See how that's eight? (Six knit stitches plus two knit together. Eight.) . . . All the way across. Work the next row plain (with no decreases), then, on the next row, make the group of stitches one less: Knit five; knit two together. Work a row plain, then, knit four, knit two together, and so on.

  Carry on in this ever-diminishing way, alternating a row of decreases with a row of plain knitting, until you are knitting two stitches together all the way across the row. Gather up the remaining stitches and admire the way the decreases spiral elegantly around the crown of the hat.

  If you want (for reasons I shudder to imagine) to make a pointy hat, just work more plain rounds between the decreasing rounds. Conversely, if you have accidentally knit a very pointy hat (which is more likely), you need fewer plain rounds to level it off.

Head sizes can be deceptive. If it's a baby head, it's a lot bigger than you think. While an adult's head is one seventh of his total body height, a baby's head is (disconcertingly) one-quarter of the total height, meaning that the proportions both around the head and from the cast-on to the crown, are more than you think. Until you have a heap of experience knitting hats (and I suggest even then), measure both the head (bigger than you think) and the knitting (smaller than you think) — often. It's hard to "eyeball" something round.

Head Rules and Exceptions

Head/hand height. The distance from the base of a person's palm to the tip of the longest finger is equal to the height of a hat (for that particular person's head) from cast-on edge (when placed just above the eyes) to the point where you begin decreasing (to shape the crown). This means that all you have to do to make a hat the right height is to lay the hand of the recipient on the knitting as the work progresses. When the knitting matches the hand height, it's time to decrease. This is a good trick to know at Christmas, when you can go around measuring hands instead of hats and make people think that they're getting mittens. (As interesting as knitting is to us, it tends to rate low in the intrigue department for non-knitters. Explaining this trick may be the best knitting moment you have all year.)

This rule doesn't not work for children under six years old (see box on page 110). And, if you don't have hands, well, handy, and you can't measure your victim, here's a rough guide to the distance to knit from cast-on to crown:

Baby	5"/13 cm
Toddler	5½"/14 cm
Child	6"/15 cm
Small adult	6½—7½"/16—19 cm
Large adult	7½—8½"/19—22 cm

VARIATIONS ON THE NO-PATTERN HAT

Rolled Brim: Simply subtract a few stitches from your starting number (maybe one inch worth) and start knitting in stockinette stitch (knitting every row). By putting a fewer stitches in the "roll" part of a roll, it will look better and stay on better. (It's still no match for a fast-moving anti-hat toddler, but it's a start.)

The beauty of the rolled-brim hat is that doing nothing actually creates a style. Most of the time you're just killing yourself for a seriously funky style, and the genius of the rolled-brim hat is that all you do is knit without thinking and whammo — it's a brim. The stockinette fabric will curl up as you go. Give yourself a little pat on the back; this curling is exactly the effect you're going for. When you have done an inch or two, add back the stitches you took away and carry on as for a standard-issue hat (following the No-Pattern Hat above).

If you're doing a rolled brim or a rolled hem or a rolled whatever, remember to let it roll while you measure for length. It sounds obvious, but instinct tells you to uncurl it the way you would to measure anything else accurately. If you don't measure it "curled," the finished piece will be annoyingly short and dorky.

Flat stockinette stitch rolls up faster than crepes at a cooking school. If this rolling bugs you, you'll have to do something else. I can assure you there's absolutely no amount of blocking that will stop it from doing this. (Go on, ask me how I know.) If you're counting on blocking to fix it, you're heading for a crushing disappointment.

Variation 2

Ribbed Edge: To work the hat with a ribbed band at the edge, first choose your ribbing style. Knit one, purl one? Make your cast-on divisible by 2. Knit three, purl one? Fudge your number so that it's divisible by 4. Your total cast-on number must be divisible by the repeat in your ribbing. Knit the ribbing so it covers the height of an ear and then carry on with the standard instructions, or knit it for double an ear's length and fold it double when you're done (for extra warmth). If you're really nervous about sizing, this can be a lifesaver: knit in ribbing all the way to the top and congratulate yourself on knitting an authentic seaman's cap.

> Ribbing has the advantage of helping hats stay on and covering the ears so they're nice and warm. The elastic, huggy nature also compensates for some minor sizing issues. If you aren't sure what size you should make a hat, make it a little big and put ribbing at the beginning. It's still no guarantee, but, then, what in knitting is?

MAKING HATS MORE EXCITING

Plain knitting can bore you silly. I wish I had something witty to say about that, but I don't. Rent a movie, listen to a book on tape, or, if the twitch over your eye gets too distracting, try one of the following solutions for jazzing up a hat.

Boring Hat Solution 1

Stripes

You'd be surprised how far stripes will go toward personalizing a hat. How about school colors, or 10 colors, or 20?

Knitting Rules!

I have never thrown away yarn. Can't do it. Some kind of sickness is what it is. I have bags of these little bits and I swear to you that other than the most basic of all philosophies — Yarn good, me keep yarn — I have no idea why I'm saving them. To deal with the guilt of all the little mini-balls of yarn hanging around the house, I knit hats with stripes. Try it. You'll feel better.

Considering how much pizzazz you can get from just picking up a different yarn every couple of rows — it's a lot of bang for your buck. It's also a wicked way to use up those little tiny bits of yarn that you've been saving. I bet you wonder why you had them.

If you're knitting a hat flat, you aren't going to have a problem matching up the stripes. Let each end hang when you change colors and use that bit to sew up that color. Weave in your ends and sew the back seam at the same time. (I won't tell you how long into my knitting life it took me to come up with that concept.)

If, however, you're knitting a hat in the round, there's going to be a teeny-weeny problem to deal with. Because knitting in the round is essentially knitting a spiral, when you change colors there's a little "step up" at the point where you change.

There are three ways that I know of to cope with this.

Ⓐ **Two words: Don't care.** Quickly develop a way to find it charming. There is absolutely nothing wrong with ignoring the "jog" that results from stripes knit in the round, especially if you move the spot where it jogs to a different spot each time. I wouldn't wear it to a knitting-guild meeting, where lots of people would feel compelled to tell me ways to avoid it, but if you really don't care, or if you actually do find it charming, then it's fine.

Ⓑ Change colors and knit the first round with your new color. When you come back to the first stitch of the new color (the first stitch of the round), pick up the stitch below it (this will be your old color), put it on the left needle in front of the first stitch of the next round, knit them together, then carry on normally. If you're not changing colors, don't do anything and knit merrily around. This technique (if you can remember to do it . . . I have some problems) hides the jog quite well.

Ⓒ You can sort of "sew away" the jog by taking the loose ends of the yarn and weaving them in afterward in the direction opposite the jog. If it's the end of the yarn on the bottom of the jog, weave it in across the jog and *up*, and if it's the loose end at the top of the jog, weave in the end across and *down*. This method doesn't hide the jog as well, but if you're feeling like a slacker, it works nicely enough. What the heck? You have to do something with the ends anyway.

Boring Hat Solution 2

Fancy Stitches

Once you've done the ribbing on a hat, there's absolutely nothing stopping you from tossing into it anything that strikes your fancy. Every pattern has a repeat whether it's Fair Isle, intarsia, or lace, and I try to choose something that's going to fit into the number of stitches I have. If I have 100 stitches, I look for something that's going to divide into that, a repeat of 2, 4, 5, 10, or 20.

If you have 100 stitches and you choose a repeating pattern that adds up to 95 or 103, take heart. You can increase or decrease the required number in the last row of ribbing. Changes that make the circumference of a hat go up or down by an inch or less will not matter, provided you have worked at least an ear size (2 inches) of ribbing first. If this rule gives you hives, always opt to make the hat bigger rather than smaller.

Pom-poms

There are knitters who frown on pom-poms. I'm one of them, and I'll freely tell you that I think much of my opposition to an enormous hairy wad of wool stuck to the top of a hat stems from the long Canadian winter when I was nine. I was, at nine years old, developing a sense of fashion. (Those who know me now will laugh at this, believing, and rightly so, that I never did develop one, but this is not the time to discuss my position on culottes.) At this time in my life I coveted, more than any other thing, a chic pink suede hat with rabbits on it that had a white satin ribbon that tied fetchingly under the chin.

My mum is a practical woman, and instead of the pink rabbit hat gracing my head (and changing my life, for the right hat can mean much for the social standing of a nine-year-old girl), I had, for that entire winter: a gray and red hand-knit hat topped with a red pom-pom on top. The pom-pom was not only red and not a rabbit (that was really its biggest crime), but it was also almost as big as my head. Since we're talking about a Canadian winter, I had to wear it, but I whipped it off and tried to hide it every time one of the pink rabbit ribbon hat girls looked my way. The pom-pom was so big that I couldn't even jam it in my pocket. The hat would go in, but the enormous pom-pom defied hiding and waggled outside of my coat. The shame and the horror have stayed with me.

That said, pom-poms do have advantages and it's not fair to let the hat hardships of my youth keep me from telling you about them.

Boring Hat Solution 4

Notions

The sewing store has a whole wall of what are called notions. Notions are pretty much anything in a fabric shop that isn't fabric, and knitters should take a long look at them. A boring hat can be improved by any number of things on that wall. You can sew on an appliqué, adorn a brim with ribbon, sew on a bow, or attach a seriously cool series of big buttons. It's a brilliant, quick solution to a lame hat, but don't forget the safety rules. If the hat is for a baby (or anyone else who might try to eat it), sew things on very securely with sewing thread, not yarn, so they aren't a choking hazard. There is no such thing as overdoing it when it comes to sewing on buttons.

WHY ISN'T THIS WORKING?

This hat is really the wrong size. You know what? I'm not going to lecture you on the evils of not swatching. I'm sure you swatched, and more than that, I'm confident that you swatched really well, and that you washed the swatch before you knit this disaster. I bet this is one of those times when the swatch lied. If the hat is well and truly too big, you have a couple of choices. Lots, actually. You can:

- **Look for a friend with a bigger head.** This is an excellent strategy for almost anything that doesn't fit. Embrace the possibility that this knitted item has a destiny that's a surprise to you. Consider the chance that even though you thought you were knitting a hat for your 10-year-old

Some knitted items have a destiny they are sworn to fulfill, regardless of your intentions. Attempting to force a skein to become something contrary to this destiny will result in revolt and perhaps a coup.

nephew, it might actually have turned out to be a hat for your great-uncle Vinny the ex-linebacker.

- **Is your hat made of plain good wool?** Could you felt it smaller? Try giving it a swish in some hot water and see what happens. Could be that you're headed for a fuzzier, but smaller, hat.

- **If you're feeling brave and bold, and have access to a sewing machine, try the "sew-and-cut" solution.** Using a sewing machine, simply sew a line down the inside of the hat. It's like "taking in" a pair of pants. After you've sewn the line, try on the hat. Small enough? If so, run another line of stitches (as insurance), then cut away the excess knitting. It's not something for the faint of heart, but it does make a smaller hat.

- **Is it possible — and I know this might seem a bit avant-garde — but is it possible that you have, in fact, not knit a hat?** Is it maybe something else?

OTHER THINGS YOUR HAT COULD BE:

- **Is it a tea cozy?** A light felting, a slit for the teapot handle, a hole for the spout and you could have something pretty, or at least unique.

- **Is it a purse?** Imagine a strap and some buttons.

- **Is it a skein of yarn?** Don't forget the ultimate solution. Undo the seams, free up the end of the yarn, and pull. Whenever I find the idea of a total do-over disheartening, I remind myself that I'm not going to use it the way it is. After a little thought (and possibly a glass or two of a decent merlot), I remember that I like yarn more than I like bad hats.

six

SOCKS

I'M KNITTING SOCKS for my husband. He's the worst kind of man to knit socks for. He has enormous feet and he likes his socks plain — no colors, no fuss, no stripes. He can occasionally be persuaded to put on socks with cables and stuff, but mostly it's round and round and round, forever and ever and ever.

When these socks are done, they'll appear ordinary, except that they're not. They are hours of my life, each one spent on him. He'll pull them on like they're run-of-the-mill footwear, they'll walk with him as he goes through his day, every day, until they wear out, and then others will take their place, these others also knit by me. It's this extraordinary ordinariness that makes socks special. That something as humdrum as socks could be elevated by love and then walked on . . . it speaks to a certain magnificence.

The truth about socks is that they're humble and beautiful and noble, and in their lowness they're the highest form of art.

FOR THE LOVE OF SOCKS

I like to think of myself as a person who is (at least in the eyes of the law and in my ability to be a parent) sane. I don't talk to myself in public (except for counting stitches or patterns); I don't rave or throw things (except when I fail to count stitches or patterns); and I hold down a job, buy groceries, and occasionally engage in normal activities like doing laundry. (I don't enjoy these activities, which I think confirms my sanity.) But none of these indications that I'm a normal, sane person with really, very little odd behavior go far toward explaining my feelings about sock yarn and knitting socks.

10 REASONS

Ten Reasons to Knit Socks

1. **They don't use much yarn.** If you're broke, knitting socks lets you come up with a finished project without having to save up like you do for a sweater's worth of yarn.

2. **They're portable.** You can tuck a ball of sock yarn in a purse or pocket and turn out knitwear wherever you go. You simply can't say the same for a sweater project or an afghan.

3. **Socks are not forever.** They're one of the only knitting projects that, if used properly, will wear out. This means, unlike with hats and scarves, you can never knit too many.

4. **Hand-knit socks are 100 percent better than store-bought.** They feel so fabulous on your feet that there's almost nobody who doesn't want to only wear hand-knit socks from the first time he slips them on.

5. There are so many ways to make socks that you can do it no matter how you like to knit; toe up, top down, on DPNs, flat, on two circulars, on one big one. If you like to knit, you'll like to knit socks.

6. Having to do the second one is good for the soul and reinforces determination and stick-to-itiveness. (Naturally, if you don't possess these qualities to begin with, this could be a downer . . .)

7. Socks have parts. This is a big help to those of us who bore easily. There's the charm of the top, the thrill of the heel, the intrigue of the instep, and the joy of shaping the toe. Helps keep interest high.

8. Once you know the rules about knitting socks, you'll never need a pattern.

9. Human feet come in a huge variety of sizes: 3½ inches for a tiny newborn, up to 12 inches for a large man. This means that no matter how badly you choke on gauge, you're going to have socks that fit someone. You might have to mail them to a basket-ball player, but they'll fit someone out there.

10. Socks are a miracle of engineering. When you knit a sock, you're doing it the same way it has always been done. You're connected with knitters over the last 700 years, all making socks and watching them wear out.

I love sock yarn. All sock yarn. Heathered sock yarn, solid sock yarn, self-patterning sock yarn, stripy sock yarn, hand-painted sock yarn — I love it all. My heart beats a little faster when I see the sock-yarn display in a yarn shop, and even if I have sworn to buy nothing, a few tiny skeins somehow sneak home with me.

I have always believed that sock yarn is the appetizer of the stash, little bits of wondrousness that we can snap up in a yarn store without it counting as buying yarn. In fact, during the few times in my life when I've decided to stop buying yarn, for reasons of economy or space, I have never extended the yarn fast to sock yarn. It's special. Don't let anybody tell you different.

In this chapter you'll find more math and technical mumbo jumbo than in the chapters on scarves, say, or hats. Don't let it scare you off. Whether you've knit a thousand socks or have never knit one at all, all of this is here to make it easier. The truth about socks is that even though they are, from an engineering point of view, remarkably complex, once you break them down to their barest elements, they're simple and straightforward, and don't even take a tape measure. Slick.

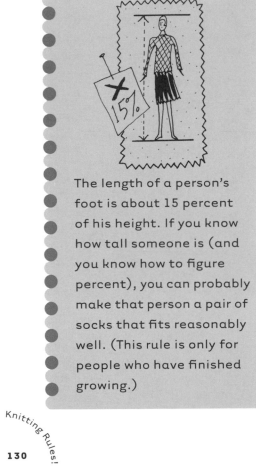

The length of a person's foot is about 15 percent of his height. If you know how tall someone is (and you know how to figure percent), you can probably make that person a pair of socks that fits reasonably well. (This rule is only for people who have finished growing.)

There are two basic approaches to sock knitting in the round. You may use a set of four or five noble, elegant double-pointed needles or you can wimp out and get some circulars. Me? I have no preference.

A Good, Plain Sock (Knit from the Cuff Down)

Once you have a basic understanding of how socks work, it's exceptionally easy to make them with no pattern at all.

Cheat Sheet

For anybody who would like to chicken out a bit, you'll find a regular sock pattern in numbered steps beginning on page 144 for a good, plain sock of exactly the sort I'm explaining in the following recipe text. If you get stuck on a part of the recipe while knitting a sock of your own design, referring to the pattern may help.

Getting Started

You know what I'm going to say and I'd like you to forgive me right now. Here it is: It all starts with gauge. Get the yarn you'd like to use and the needles you'd like to use and knit a swatch to figure out how many stitches you have per inch. Measure the leg at the place where the calf muscle ends, multiply this by the gauge, and cast on.

Number of stitches per inch (*slightly stretched*) × number of inches around your leg = number of stitches to cast on

I always stretch the swatch for socks a little bit before I measure it. I find that if I cast on the right number to go around my leg, my socks fall down. Using a few stitches less (maybe an inch worth) keeps me from having my regular fashion problems compounded by perpetually wearing slouch socks.

Don't use the "knitted-on cast-on" for socks. The sturdy firm edge it produces is fine for many things, but it won't stretch enough for most people to wear a sock comfortably. Try the long-tail cast-on (see glossary) or casting on over two needles so the stitches are bigger and you get a really stretchy top. That said, if you don't care for the person you're knitting for, or if you have always been curious, simply from a scientific perspective, about what it takes to cut off the circulation to a human foot, go right ahead.

The more tightly knit a yarn is, the better it holds up. Any room left in between the stitches allows the fibers to abrade against each other, causing undue wear and tear. This is a good enough reason to knit socks at a slightly tighter gauge (more stitches to the inch) than you would usually be partial to. If you love to darn socks, ignore me, but do send me your address so I can mail you the family's socks with holes in 'em.

Sock Leg

Once I work out how many stitches to cast on, I work in ribbing for a while. By "a while" I mean an inch or two or three, depending on my preference, and yours. Knitting

> Adjust the number of stitches that you're casting on to fit the kind of ribbing you'd like. Knit 2, purl 2 rib needs a multiple of 4, whereas knit 1, purl 1 requires a multiple of 2. When adjusting the total number by a stitch or two, adjust downward or the socks won't stay up.

goddess Elizabeth Zimmermann had it pegged when she suggested that you work on ribbing until you're sick of it. You'd be surprised how often that works out to be the exact length you need.

For reasons I've never understood, knit 2, purl 2 ribbing seems to stay up the best, but knit 1, purl 1 looks the snappiest. Choose your priorities.

If you get tired of ribbing, change to stockinette stitch and carry on until the sock is a length that amuses you, fits your victim, or is the approximate length of your hand, palm base to fingertip.

If you knit sock tops that measure the same distance as the length of the leg from the bottom of the calf muscle to the top of the heel, you don't need calf shaping, just a tube. For mathematically challenged types like me, this is a good idea.

FIVE WAYS TO MAKE SOCK KNITTING MORE EXCITING

There is very little I can tell you about hanging in there over the long, boring bits of socks. The following have helped me get past the monotony of knitting down to the heel.

1. **Self-patterning or otherwise amusing yarn.** I'm apparently dim enough to be entertained by waiting for the discovery of what color will turn up next with variegated yarn.

2. **The reward system.** Every 5 or 10 rows, give yourself a treat, like a square of chocolate. This is a temporary solution at best, though; if you adopt it for too long, you'll gain so much weight that your socks won't fit you anymore.

3. **Movies.** Rent 'em.

4. **Take your socks everywhere.** A round on the bus, a round on the phone, a quickie while you make dinner: It adds up. I churn out several pairs a year while waiting in line. Stick that sucker in your bag and look for opportunity.

5. **Books on tape.** Since I started getting these, my whole knitting world has changed. I'm finally getting to all those classics I so want to discuss at parties and the socks are flying off the needles.

The Heel Flap

I like me a decent flap heel. I think they're easy, durable, and without flaw. There are proponents I know of the short row, hourglass, or peasant heel, and to humor them I've made other heels. You should try a bunch of them and then decide for yourself, but know I prefer the flap, and I've thought a lot about it.

For a flap heel, you don't need a tape measure. Simply make the flap on half the stitches and continue until it's a square. Nifty, eh?

All standard heels are worked on half of the stitches. This is true of the flap heel, the short row heel, and most others I've met. There are reasons to do them on less or more (like having heels on your body that are unusually narrow or wide), but half is a good starting place and will fit most of humanity.

Put half the stitches onto one needle. Let the others be; we aren't concerned with them for the next little bit. Choose one of the following methods and notice that each option for a heel flap has every row starting with a slipped stitch. You want that. It makes your life (well, your knitting life) easier later.

Method 1 **Standard, no-screwing-around, straight-up heel.** Work back and forth, always slipping the first stitch of every row, knitting the right-side rows, purling the wrong-side rows. Carry on bravely until the flap is a square.

Method 2 **Sturdy heel.** Right-side rows: Slip one, knit one all the way across, ending with a knit. Wrong-side rows: Slip one, purl the rest of the way. Continue until the flap is a square.

If you want your life to be easy, work heels on an even number of stitches. A decrease worked in the middle of the first row of the heel will solve the problem if you have an odd number.

Method 3 **Eye of partridge heel.** Row 1 (RS): * Slip 1, knit 1; repeat from * to end of row. Row 2: Slip 1, purl to end of row. Row 3: Slip 1, *slip 1, knit 1; repeat from * to last stitch; knit 1. Row 4: Repeat Row 2. Repeat Rows 1–4 until the flap is a square.

Turning the Heel

When you have a flap that is a square, you'll perform the actual turning of the heel. Turning the heel is a mythic act, one that sock knitters speak of with reverence. Turning the heel is when you, through an incredibly simple but clever series of short rows (see glossary), make the sock change direction and move from leg to foot. I've done a hundred socks and I feel smart every time.

With the right side of the work facing you, begin by counting your stitches — I'm not going to help you with that; it's insulting — and make careful note of your center stitch. With that in mind, you're going to knit to "a few" past the center stitch (see box below), then knit two together, knit one, and turn your work around. Now the wrong side is facing you and you need to count how many stitches were left when you turned around and give it a think. You want the same number left over this time. Slip one, purl until you are three stitches away from that number; purl two together, purl one, and turn your work. If all has gone well, you'll have a center group of stitches you just worked and an equal number of stitches on either side of that group, with a gap separating the just-worked and not-yet-worked stitches on either side. (Take note of that gap.) If you do, congratulations. You are home free. If not, take a deep breath, figure out if you need to knit more or fewer to make it equal, then eat a bonbon and try again.

Don't think too much about this. Simply make an equal number of stitches on either side of the worked group in the center. The goal is to have the center group measure about 1 inch (2 cm).

From here, all a knitter needs to do to have a brilliant heel is continue back and forth, slipping the first stitch, working to one stitch before the gap, working two stitches together over the gap, then working one stitch, and turning, until all of the heel stitches are used up.

The number of stitches in the middle of the group determines how deep or shallow the heel will be. If you are knitting for someone with a broad heel, add a few more to the middle. On the other side of the coin, if the recipient has narrow (or pointy) heels, make the center group smaller.

A Quick Game of Pickup

Take a deep breath, find yourself some good lighting, and get ready to pick up stitches along the sides of the heel flap. Remember how much I talked about slipping the first stitch of every row when you were doing the flap? Looking down the sides of the flap, you'll see a chain of larger stitches, the result of the slipped stitches. These are your instep stitches waiting to be picked up.

Using your free needle, scoop up all of these stitches and then knit them. As unbelievable as it may sound, this will be the right number of stitches to pick up. Just go get each of those long stitches along the side and try not to look too smug: It makes the other knitters want to smack you. Knit across the regular stitches that are in your way and do the same thing on the other side.

After you have all the flap stitches picked up, knit half of the heel stitches onto the needle with the second set of picked-up stitches. If all has gone well (and what could have gone wrong?), you'll be making a tube again. Number your needles 1, 2, and 3. On needle 1 there should be half of your heel stitches and the first set of newcomers. On needle 2 are all of your stitches for the top of the foot. On needle 3 are the other new stitches and the other half of the heel. Welcome to the foot. You're going to love it here.

Making it to this point always seems like halfway to me. I suppose that whether or not it's technically halfway depends on how long the leg and foot are, but spiritually I always give myself a little pat on the back at this juncture.

Gussets at the Instep

Remember numbering your needles 1, 2, and 3? If you admire your sock at this stage, which is something I do all through the process, you can see that the stitches for the bottom of the foot are on needles 1 and 3 and the stitches for the top of the foot are on needle 2.

After picking up the flap stitches, you will have way too many stitches. You need to decrease back down to the number you cast on in the first place. I feel bad pointing this out because you're so clever, but I have to do it. If you decrease down to fewer stitches than you cast on, you'll make a foot that is narrower than normal. If you don't decrease that far and have more stitches than you cast on, the foot will be wider than normal. Take a look at your feet and think it through. Are your feet normal, wide, or narrow?

Since it would be weird-looking to run the decreases along the top and uncomfortable to put them along the bottom where you would walk on them, the decreases in socks run along the sides.

When decreasing the stitches for the gusset, you have to contemplate only the three stitches on each side of the bottom of the sock. There will be three at the end of needle 1, and three at the beginning of needle 3. The decreases are worked on these stitches every other row, like this (see box page 144 on ssk):

Needle 1 (bottom of the foot): Knit to last 3 stitches, K2tog, K1.
Needle 2 (top of the foot): Work, doing nothing.
Needle 3: K1, ssk, knit to the end.
Alternate this round with a plain round of knitting until you are back down to your original number of stitches.

When you're done with your decreases, you should have the same number for the top of the foot (needle 2) as you do for the bottom (needles 1 and 3). If you're a few off, you can rig it a little by fudging a decrease here or there. If you're off by a lot, you need a friend with feet as odd as fish.

Figuring Foot Length

The length of a person's foot measures pretty much the same as that person's forearm — that is, elbow to wristbone. Aside from that being an interesting piece of information, it's a secret weapon for sneaky sock knitters everywhere. Armed with this knowledge, you can measure the recipient's arm without tipping him off to your intentions to knit him socks; though it may get him hopeful for a sweater.

If you know the recipient's shoe size, the chart below might save you in a pinch.

Range	Shoe size	Length
Baby	0	3"/8 cm
Kids	2	4"/10 cm
Kids	5	5"/13 cm
Kids	8	6"/15 cm
Kids	11	7"/18 cm
Women's extra small	3	8"/20 cm
Women's small	6	9"/23 cm
Women's medium	9	10"/25 cm
Women's large	12	11"/28 cm
Men's small	5	9"/23 cm
Men's medium	8	10"/25 cm
Men's large	11	11"/28 cm
Men's extra large	14	12"/30 cm

Something is Afoot . . .

Really, all that remains at this point is more of the monotonous round and round that you did on the leg — and, of course, knowing when to stop. If you can try on the sock, that works best. Quit knitting and start working the toe when the sock fits down to the base of your toes, or 1¼ inches (3 cm) before you want to end the sock.

Make the Toe

Because human feet are not square (at least not usually — if yours are, I'm sorry I mentioned it; my condolences), when you get to the toe you're going to want to taper off. This is where the business about having top-of-foot and bottom-of-foot stitches pays off again. You're going to decrease at the sides of the feet again. Looking at all of your stitches, concern yourself with the six at each side of the foot. These will be: the last three stitches on needle 1, the first and last three stitches on needle 2, and the first three stitches on needle 3.

With this in mind, knit to the three stitches in the corner, knit two together, and knit one. Move to the top of the foot, knit one, ssk, knit to the last three stitches, knit two together, knit one.

Last needle, knit one, ssk, knit to the end of the needle.

Alternate this round of decreases with rounds of plain knitting.

Decrease until you have a toe that either looks right or is about one quarter the total width of the foot.

Cast off and sew together, work a three-needle bind-off, or — and this is really the right way to do it — Kitchener or graft the toe shut.

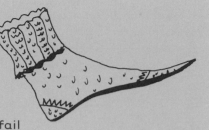

How to avoid pointy toes? Most sock toes want to be pointy. I find this frustrating, as I have short, squat peasant feet that aspire to pointiness but fail miserably. Years of experimentation (and failed attempts to make my feet pointier . . . don't ask) have led to the following: I knit the decreases (or increases for toe-up socks) until the last two or first two rows with decreases every other row, then decrease every row the last (or first) two. Voilà. Less pointy, less elegant toes. (But I'm not bitter.)

Kitchener stitch (or grafting, depending on where you live and who taught you) is a way of weaving together two pieces of knitting such that you have an absolutely seamless join. Look in any of your books, ask at the knitting shop, or, if you really want to know how to do it, try this. Stand in the presence of another knitter who you know is serious about sock knitting. Wait until there's a lull in the conversation, then say loudly, "There has to be a better way to finish sock toes." Someone will teach you instantly.

Grafting takes some heat for being sort of difficult. Try to let go of this and not believe what other knitters tell you before you try it for yourself. Remember how things were in high school and don't give a technique a hard time because it has a reputation. (For a start, see the basic explanation in the glossary on page 214.)

There are a lot of ways to do things.
Think outside the box and
be in charge of your knitting.
With wool as my witness, and despite
how that lady treated you
in the yarn shop that one time,

there are no
knitting police.

Do what you want.

STEP-BY-STEP CHEAT SHEET FOR SOCKS

This standard pair of socks will fit an average woman. They are knit out of sock yarn, using 2.5 mm needles at a gauge of 7.5 stitches to the inch in stockinette stitch.

An ssk is a way to knit two together slanting to the left (the opposite way than usual). To work it, slip one, slip a second one, then put your left needle in the front of these two and knit them together.

1. Cast on 64 stitches and join in a round without twisting. Knit for 2 inches in "knit 2, purl 2" ribbing. Then change to plain stockinette and work until the sock leg measures 7 inches or you simply can't go on.

2. Heel flap: Put half the stitches (32) on one needle and continue as follows. Right side: *Sl1, K1: repeat from * to the end; wrong side: slip 1, purl to the end.
   Repeat these two rows 14 times until the heel flap is a square. End by working a wrong-side row and have the right side facing you.

3. With right side facing, Sl1, K17, ssk (see box above), K1, turn. Sl1, P5, P2tog, P1, turn.
   Sl1, K6, ssk, K1, turn. Sl1, P7, P2tog, P1, turn.
   Continue in this fashion, slipping the first stitch, working to one stitch before the gap, working 2 sts together over the gap, then knit 1 (or purl 1) until you finish all the heel stitches. Eighteen stitches remain.

4. **Needle 1:** Knit heel sts, pick up 16 sts up side of heel.
   Needle 2: K32 for top of foot.
   Needle 3: Pick up 16 sts down side of heel, knit first 9 heel sts (82 sts in all).

Knitting Rules!

5 Round 1:

Needle 1: Knit to 3 sts before the end of needle, K2tog, Knit to end.

Needle 2: Knit plain to end of needle.

Needle 3: K1, ssk, knit to end.

Round 2: Knit plain all the way around.

Repeat rounds 1 and 2 until you have 64 sts (divided 16, 32, 16).

6 Continue knitting plain, around and around, until the sock measures 5 inches from the picked-up stitches.

7 Round 1:

Needle 1: Knit to last 3 stitches, K2tog, K1.

Needle 2: K1, ssk, knit to last 3 stitches, K2tog, K1.

Needle 3: K1, ssk, knit to end of needle.

Round 2: Knit to end of round.

Repeat rounds 1 and 2 until 16 stitches remain.

Graft two sets of 8.

Whenever you're knitting socks among other knitters, they come up to you and hold a mini-conference. Do you knit them on DPNs or on two circulars? Do you work decreases every row or every other row? Do you do left- or right-leaning decreases or both? Everybody has an opinion, and everyone knows the best way to do everything. I've always found that the best thing to do when people tell you how to knit (including me) is to listen with a smile, consider what you think makes sense, and then do it your way. Nobody has ever been struck by lightning for ignoring knitting advice. Occasionally there are really weird results, but never any third-degree burns.

FIVE VARIATIONS ON THE BASIC SOCK

Variation 1

Stripes. Alternate two, five, eight colors. You decide.

Variation 2

Texture. There's no end to the entertaining ways that you can toss cables and textured stitches into socks. I try to keep in mind two things before I go nuts. First, cables make a sock narrower, so I have to remember to add a few extra stitches or I'm making that four-year-old down the street another pair by accident. Second, I try to remember not to put the texture on the bottom of the foot. It takes only 10 minutes of walking around on bobbles to learn that one.

Variation 3

Choose a Fair Isle pattern and toss it in there. Fudge the stitch count to make it work. Remember, Fair Isle isn't as stretchy, so don't scale the stitch count downward unless you don't especially care for the recipient and would like to pox him with absolutely beautiful warm socks that he can't get on.

Variation 4

Lace. Choose a lace pattern from the stitch dictionary and get going. Lace is usually elastic, so if you're changing your number to cast on by a few stitches to make the lace work, you can go downward. If you're going to do lace socks, think about working the lace only on the top of the foot. Sock bottoms work best in plain, sturdy stitches.

Variation 5

Try one of the other million (okay, maybe not a million) ways to make socks. Knit them toe up, flat, on circulars, with the "magic loop"; with a handkerchief heel, an hourglass heel, a short row heel. Try self-patterning yarns or solid yarns; fingering or chunky weight; mohair or cashmere or good old sheepy wool. Do a zillion things, keep your eyes open, and ask other knitters what they do.

For the love of socks, heed this advice: Once you finish the first sock, always cast on the second sock right away. It improves the chances of getting a pair.

WHY ISN'T THIS WORKING?

My socks start out the right size and then grow bigger as I wear them. What's going wrong?

The gauge is too loose. Go down a couple of needle sizes and try again. In the meantime, you can felt the ones you made, or mail them to my husband. He has huge feet.

My socks are doing this stupid loose thing at the ankle.

If socks bag and droop at the ankles, you need shaping. Much like bagging and drooping in humans, this can be avoided by doing a little decreasing. Knit a leg as you would normally, then, about an inch from the anklebone and the start of the heel, decrease by a few stitches. Knit the heel as you would normally, then when decreasing over the instep, work back to your original cast-on number. If this sounds like too much bother, do as I do and cop out and knit ribbing all the way down. It's a quick fix, but it works better than math some days.

In the spots where I change needles, there's a loose line of stitches. What is that and how do I make it go away?

If you want to look slick in a sock-knitting circle then you call those *ladders*. There's a bunch of ways to make them go away, all of which are hotly contested.

- Tug firmly on the first stitch of every needle to tighten up that little gap.
- Work on circulars so you don't have needles to gap between.
- Try knitting with a set of five needles instead of four (two for the top stitches, two for the bottom). This sets the stitches in a square instead of a triangle and there's a greater angle between stitches, which seems to help some knitters avoid ladders.
- Wind the yarn in the opposite direction when knitting the first stitch on the needle (that is, clockwise instead of counterclockwise). This makes a knit stitch that sits sort of twisted on the needle, but like all twisted stitches, it's tighter than its buddies. When you come back to this stitch on the next round, insert your needle into the front of the stitch to untwist it, then wrap the yarn around clockwise to twist the one you're making. With practice, you'll do this automatically, though for the first several months it can drive you batty.
- Work a lace pattern, so you can't see the stupid ladders.

Skeins of sock yarn are small enough that many hundreds may be squirreled away in your home without revealing the true scope of your addiction. Look for discreet, infrequently visited locations . . . the pockets of luggage, tucked inside a gravy boat, behind books on bookshelves, or in the extra space in the corners of the guest-room pillowcases.

SOCKS FOR YOUR SOUL

Recently, a friend was going through a difficult time. It was an ugly divorce, he missed his children, and nothing seemed to lighten him. In desperation, I mailed him a pattern for kilt hose, old-fashioned steel needles and some good sock-weight wool. He was stunned. He didn't know how to knit, and here I was suggesting that he go from absolute non-knitter status to full-blown, fine-gauge, men's socks. He thought I was nuts, but agreed to try.

The stuff arrived at his house in the morning and that entire afternoon went down the drain as he sat down and taught himself to cast on. By dinnertime, he was knitting. I don't think I could say he was knitting well, and I don't think he liked me very much that day, but he was knitting. Probably the sanity of both of us was in doubt.

Meanwhile, I was sure knitting would help him. I really thought having small successes every day, things he was in charge of — even though they were only stitches — could help. I thought his ego could use an opportunity to be productive in a way he could see, and that he needed a chance to make mistakes without dire consequences. I believed, and he must have believed too or he wouldn't have spent umpteen hours humoring the crazy knitting lady, that this could help him feel better.

It's way too soon to tell if knitting kilt hose was a good idea or just a stupid missionary move on my part. I tell you this, though; I bet you're wondering right now if it worked, and that means something. That means you think sock knitting *could* change someone's path and make him feel better. That means you think knitting socks matters . . . despite how dumb it seems to try it.

10 REASONS

Ten Reasons Not to Knit Socks

Ordinarily I'd never write a list like this, but there are problems with socks, and it's only fair that you know this up front so you walk in (ha!) with your eyes wide open.

1. Sock knitting may be addictive.

2. Knitting socks can lead to an obsession with any form of footwear. It may be a gateway to other uncontrollable knitting, like slippers and, in the very vulnerable, men's knee-high kilt hose.

3. Once you knit a pair for someone, there is a 96 percent probability that you will be not only asked but continuously implored as well, to provide him with a lifetime of hand-knit socks. If this person is young, this could be a lot of socks.

4. Sock yarn is a mysterious animal. For reasons that I can't explain, very few knitters count it as actual "stash." A few balls here, a few balls there, and the next thing you know, you're thinking about having the kids keep their clothes in the garage to give you more yarn space.

5. Sock yarn is inexpensive enough that the problem of reason 4 is not curbed by a decrease in income.

6 There are two socks in a pair. This means that after you have knit one sock (forgive me for being obvious), you must knit another one, and it has to be exactly the same. If you're an easily bored knitter, it could be that you're going to wear a lot of mismatched socks from now on.

7 Sock needles are sharp. Untidy knitters who leave their knitting lying around would do well to note that a puncture wound arising from a sock-knitting "incident" (and don't pretend that you're above it) requires a tetanus shot. (I advise getting one just in case when you take up with socks. Saves time.)

8 Once you knit socks, you'll have to deal with a lifetime of explaining to people why you bother. They'll point out that socks from the store are two bucks a pair and you'll counterargue with a gift of a hand-knit pair of socks to help them understand. (See reason 3 for the problem that exists beyond this bugging the daylights out of you.)

9 Sock yarn may be the knitter's version of methadone. It's what you buy when you don't really want to buy a lot of yarn, or when you just need to take the edge off. It's dangerous, easy, and comes in irresistible self-patterning varieties that make you feel clever.

10 There are so many kinds of socks that no matter what you're thinking now, once you start, you'll never be able to stop.

seven

SCARVES AND SHAWLS

I'M A STATISTICAL ANOMALY in the knitting world. I'm one of only an apparent handful of knitters who didn't learn to knit by cutting their stitching teeth on a scarf. (It was a pot holder. I was four. I didn't have what it takes to get through a scarf.) Perhaps my grandmother intended for me to knit a scarf, but then she realized my attention span was that of a tsetse fly and figured out a way for me to bail. Or, maybe my disdain for scarves as a teaching tool is genetic. For whatever reason, it was years and years before I knit one, and I'm still not convinced that scarves are for beginners.

SCARF BASICS

Scarves are a decent commitment, and I don't understand why we refer to beginning knitters as being in "the scarf stage," as though they're larval knitters, not yet fully aware or awake. I don't know if anybody has noticed yet, but a lot of these "scarf-stage" knitters are turning out square yardage that would awe a seasoned knitter — and are becoming extraordinarily adept in the process. In addition, many of these knitters are using yarns that are darn tricky. These fun fur, fancy-pants novelty yarns are harder to work with than you think, and though you could conceivably knit a quick and easy scarf using the fuzzy skeins, even an experienced knitter has to admit that it's difficult to knit a freakin' stitch if you can't find it on the needle. I know knitters who've been beaten by the sheer volume and monotony of a scarf, or been reduced to gibbering idiots by a lace pattern so complex that signing up for dental experiments at the local veterinary college would seem like a better hobby.

10
REASONS

Ten Reasons to Knit a Scarf

1. Everybody needs one. If you live in a warm place, a scarf is an accessory; if you live in a cold place (like Canada), it's a necessity — all that stands between you and certain death. (Okay, not certain death. Frostbite maybe; chilliness for sure.)

2. A friend of mine likes to say that a winter scarf is "caulking." Wound round your neck it bridges the difficult gap a coat leaves at the top and keeps all your heat from escaping.

3. No matter how many coats you own, by the time January rolls around, you'll be sick to death of all of them. Owning 20 scarves adds a little color to the endless winter and lets you pretend that you have a different look.

4. You can skip the gauge swatch with a scarf and have it matter not at all. How could a scarf not fit? (Don't answer that. I'm sure I'll find out.)

(5) Scarves are varied in technical difficulty. You can do one in a plain garter stitch, or make a delicate lace wonder. You could knit nothing but scarves your whole knitting career, never repeat yourself, and learn almost every knitting technique.

(6) Scarves are easy, at least mostly easy. If you're a beginning knitter, you can get a fabulous yarn and let it do all the work.

(7) Just as there's comfort food, there's comfort knitting, and a nice plain scarf out of simple delicious wool, knit back and forth in naïve, mindless rows, is good for those days when anything more complex would make you cry.

(8) A scarf is always a welcome gift. Even if the recipient lives in Hawaii, a scarf made of a wee slip of silk will be gratefully received.

(9) If say, you were going to rob a bank (not that you would, that would be wrong) a scarf could be a vital part of your disguise.

(10) The scarf is the gateway to the shawl. There are only so many scarves you can knit before you feel an urge in the shawl direction.

Whatever it is, scarves are not the simple rectangles we think of when we remember our early knitting days. They are, instead, a medium for knitters to play in that has virtually no limits. (That was intended to be inspirational. Go knit a scarf.)

HOW CREATIVE CAN YOU BE?

Imagine a scarf as an unlimited canvas. Do you imagine a 12-foot garter-stitch behemoth that any Inuit would envy? Do it. How about a wee bit of lace, just big enough to peek out of the top of a woolen coat? There's no reason not to invent, play, or try anything you can see in your mind's eye; it's not like you're going to have to figure out how your plan affects the scarf's armholes. If you can knit it, you can wear it. (Admittedly, and there's no point in pretending this isn't true, there are regrettable scarves. Still, there's much less chance that a fitting error or misunderstanding of the human form will stand in the way of your brilliance.)

I feel quite bad now — having said in an earlier chapter that a hat is a much better project for a beginners — that I'm going to sing the praises of a scarf as a project for a novice knitter. Not a very beginning knitter — because I think that a scarf just goes on too long for someone who struggles for every stitch and really needs the satisfaction of something finished to feel like a knitter — but for someone trying to learn

> The scarf is the ultimate tool for knitterly self-expression. With a minimum of skill and understanding, you can make something that (for better or worse) will be unique. Go forth and knit.

How Big Should It Be?

This is one of the reasons I like scarves. Unlike sweaters and hats, the answer to "How big do I make it?" is always "As big as you want." If it will go around your neck in any way, it's a scarf. If, however, you're feeling somewhat traditional, or just want a hint for where to begin (or end), the chart below lists the expected sizes of store-bought scarves.

To do your own figuring for length of an ordinary scarf intended for warmth, a good starting place is the wearer's height. For a person who's six feet tall, make the scarf six feet long. If you want it to wrap around the neck several times, start with the height and add 12 to 16 inches (30–40 cm) of length for each wrap.

What kind of scarf?	Normal width	Normal length
Men's traditional dress scarf	12"/30 cm	60"/152 cm
Long winter scarf (to wrap around your neck once or twice)	10"/30 cm	At least 80"/ 203 cm
Women's small tuck-in scarf	8"/20 cm	40"/101 cm

something, a scarf can provide undeniable glory. Scarves are a great way to learn something new. You can try any technique on a scarf and be able to focus on the one new element you're learning. New to cables? A cabled scarf frees you from the worries of gauge, of incorporating sleeve increases into the pattern, or, in my case, of the obsessive urge to mirror cables properly on the right and left sides of a sweater front.

Cabling, lace, grafting, colorwork: a scarf provides a flat, broad canvas on which to knit. Think of a scarf as a really big swatch you can wear.

HOW MUCH YARN DO YOU NEED?

When I want to knit a scarf, I get what I like out of the stash (or, for the stash impaired, you could go to a yarn shop but I suggest getting lots while you're at it, so you have your own yarn shop at home, should the urge to knit a scarf strike you at 1 A.M.). When I buy scarf yarn, I buy as much as I think I'll need. If it's a big scarf, I get a lot; if it's a wee thing, I get a little, maybe just one skein. I don't worry about whether I'm right about it, because I don't mind the scarf presenting a small surprise. If it turns out to be longer than expected, I can stop. If it's shorter, I can call it a "tuck-in" and stop. It's only when I want the project to be a specific size (or I'm trying to give my brother Ian a manly cabled scarf that does more than barely tuck under his chin) that I give a little thought to what amount I should have.

Never trust how much yarn someone says to get. (Especially don't trust me. As careful as I am with these things, I feel that, in the interest of full disclosure, I should tell you I failed grade-10 math three times, and I'm somewhat mathematically challenged.) No matter who tells you — me, a pattern, your aunt Sheila — if you're really, really worried about having enough yarn, *get an extra ball for insurance.* Theoretically, you can return the extra ball to the store if you don't need it, but I've never heard of anyone doing that.

BASIC SCARF YARDAGE

The chart below details, in the vaguest way possible, how much yarn (of various weights) I think you'd need for a scarf knit in stockinette stitch. Garter stitch and cables are going to take a little more; lacework, a little less.

Most of the time you're knitting a scarf from end to end, so you're not going to run out of yarn: You're going to finish. When the yarn is gone, you're out of there. Be flexible.

Scarf size	Chunky	Worsted	Dk/sport	Fingering
12"×60" 30×150 cm	300 yards/ 215 m	400 yards/ 365 m	520 yards/ 475 m	540 yards/ 495 m
10"×80" 25×200 cm	330 yards/ 300 m	445 yards/ 410 m	575 yards/ 525 m	600 yards/ 550 m
8"×40" 20×100 cm	130 yards/ 120 m	175 yards/ 160 m	230 yards/ 210 m	240 yards/ 220 m

THREE SCARVES AND MUCH OF WHAT YOU NEED TO KNOW

I really believe that if you understand the following three scarf recipes, you should be able to use them as jumping-off places to launch the scarf of your dreams. Cables, lace, stripes . . . one of these ideas should give you the framework from which to achieve leap acclamation, stardom, and fame. Knitters will fall at your feet and search for words while tears run down their rosie cheeks as they attempt to explain just a fraction of what it means tothem to see that your idea has sprung forth from your mind and been made real in the context of wool. They will . . .

I'm sorry. Really sorry. I get excited.

The most clever scarf knitter in the world is a genius, a visionary, a woman so smart that her intellect is dangerous. She has had the best ideas for scarves the world has ever seen. She is so clever, so creative, so innovative that sometimes when she has these ideas she can scarcely believe it herself. Do you know who she is? *No.* That's my point. There *is* no scarf fame. There are, however, some great scarves, and, damnit, you can invent one. (Cue the music and bring me my cape.)

A plain scarf doesn't have to be. Open your stitch dictionary, choose a stitch you like, and try that. Remember, patterns that combine knit and purl lie flat and stitches based on stockinette don't. If you want to use a pattern you think is going to curl, simply add a border in garter stitch (or another flat pattern) on both sides. It'll help.

The Starting Place Scarf

This is a simple scarf, knit from one end to the other. It's plain vanilla, it's oatmeal in the morning, it's the opposite of a lace-cashmere mantilla. (Though with the help of a good stitch dictionary and a lace edging, it could be one . . .) It's the most basic scarf in the universe and the only serious skill needed is perseverance, because things can get a little boring. (Actually, things can get a lot boring, though I prefer to think of it as *meditative.*)

Ingredients

Get your yarn and the needles you might use with that weight (*Hint:* It tells you on the ball band).

How to Do It

1. Look on the label for the suggested gauge and figure out how many stitches to the inch you're likely to get. If the ball band says the yarn works at 20 stitches to 4 inches, then 20 divided by 4 equals 5 stitches to the inch.

2. Decide how wide you want the scarf to be. If you want it to be 8 inches wide, for example, multiply 8 by the number of stitches to the inch: 8 inches wide × 5 stitches to the inch = 40 stitches total, and that's how many you cast on.

> **Width of scarf (in inches) × number of stitches to the inch = number of stitches to cast on**

3. Now knit (or whatever stitch you want to use) every stitch, every row, until you run out of yarn, and then cast off.

You can substitute any stitch pattern you like into a plain scarf pattern, but each is going to change the finished size and shape of your scarf. Remember that lace tends to spread wider than stockinette, cables pull in more than stockinette, and any pattern you put into a scarf tends to stretch lengthwise as it's pulled by gravity on the wearer. (This last point is actually fairly important; failure to compensate for gravity is the leading cause of painful post-knitting lengthening and excess-scarf-length injuries and dorkiness.) Allow for a scarf to grow a little, or if it's a long, long scarf — a lot.

VARYING YOUR STITCH

Different stitch patterns are based on different numbers of stitches, so check how many stitches your pattern is a multiple of, and make the adjustments to your total stitch count. For example: You look in a stitch dictionary and pick a pretty lace pattern that's a repeat of 7. You know you want your scarf about 8 inches wide and you're getting 5 stitches to the inch, so you're going to cast on about 40 stitches for plain knitting. What number near 40 is a multiple of 7? Well, there's 35 or 42.

The pattern I've chosen is based on stockinette (knit one side, purl the other), which is going to curl, so I need a border to make it lie flat. Well, let's add 3 stitches on each side for borders, a total of 6. If I go with 42 stitches, the total to cast on will be: 42 + 6 (for border) = 48.

That's a few more stitches than I wanted, plus it's a lacy pattern, so nope. That's a setup for a one-way ticket to Crazytown. I'll go with the 35, for a total of: 35 + 6 = 41, only one stitch off of my original stitch count.

Knitting Rules!

I could even go down one more multiple of 7, but I think a slightly too wide scarf is better than a slightly too skinny one. I might feel differently if I lived somewhere with less snow.

Thinking In Another Direction

If Scarf Recipe #1 is like oatmeal, this one is like . . . well, it's still like oatmeal. It's basically the same scarf but knit side to side instead of end to end. This scarf is a relief for knitters who hate turning at the ends of rows, enjoy the commitment of a row that goes on for a good long time, and think that casting on and off many, many stitches in a single go is a day at the beach.

Ingredients

The yarn of choice and needles long enough to hold all the stitches. It's going to be a lot, so you might want to work back and forth on a circular instead of straights.

Because you're knitting lengthwise, this scarf can make lengthwise stripes. I often think of this one when I'm looking to use up odd balls from my collection. If you change yarns every row or two, you can simply begin and end your new rows on alternate sides, let the ends hang free, and knot them up when you're done to get a simple fringe that gets you out of weaving in the ends. Obviously, if you hate fringe and loathe weaving in ends, this is probably not the project for you. Don't say I didn't warn you.

How to Do It

1 Decide how long you'd like the scarf to be. Using the math from Scarf Recipe #1, and substituting length for width, figure:

> **Length of scarf (in inches) × number of stitches to the inch = number of stitches to cast on**

2 Cast on the desired number and off you go.

3 Knit along until the scarf is as wide as you'd like it to be, then cast off.

The Middle Ground

A Scarf with Lace Edges

I love this scarf because it solved a problem that had been bugging me. Most lace patterns have a "this-end-up" element to them and they don't look the same right-side up as they do upside down. It used to annoy the daylights out of me when I knit a scarf with lace edges from end to end and I admired it and loved it — until somebody put it on. Then, suddenly, one end of the lace would appear upside down on the wearer. (If you're the sort of person who is laughing at me right now for caring about silly things like not having the ends of my scarf match, then move along. We'll make a deal. You won't pick on those of us who need things to be matching in order to sleep at night, and we won't laugh at your upside-down lace.)

Ingredients

Yarn and the needles of your choice.

How to Do It

1 Choose a lace pattern from your stitch dictionary and work out the number to cast on (allowing a number that accommodates the repeats of the lace pattern), as described in Scarf Recipe #1 (see page 162).

2 Knit the lace pattern for a bit, then switch to garter stitch (or something else that lies flat) until half the yarn is gone or the scarf is half the length you'd like it to be. Put the stitches on a stitch holder or slide them to the back of your circular needle.

3 Break the yarn. Now, begin with step 1 again to produce a second scarf "half" that's just like the first one.

4 When you're finished, graft (or sew, if you're a chicken) the two pieces together. Voilà: a scarf that has two matching ends. What a relief.

A VARIATION INSPIRED BY NECESSITY

Recently I spent an obscene amount of money on a single perfect, exquisite skein of hand-dyed silk. (No, I'm not sorry, and yes, it was very beautiful.) I didn't want to waste a single yard. (It was expensive enough that you'd be able to calculate the dollar value of the wasted yarn and never stop thinking about it.)

The pattern suggested (well, it didn't really suggest, it directed, but I believe that all patterns are just guidelines) that you knit three inches of a lacy pattern, then 36 inches of seed stitch, then repeat the lacy bit. I wasn't thrilled with the plan. To my way of reckoning, 36 inches might leave leftovers, and there was no way I was having leftovers. It would be like not staying for dessert on a date with Johnny Depp. I thought about lengthening the scarf, but how was I going to know by how much? I couldn't just knit until I ran out of yarn because of the three inches of lace on the end, and I didn't want to employ my usual method of grafting in the middle because I still didn't know where the middle of the skein was, and because it makes me a little delirious to graft seed stitch. (Note that I didn't say I *can't* graft seed stitch. It's only knitting; I can do anything. I just choose not to, that's all, the same way I choose not to lie in the middle of the freeway or file my teeth into points.) I was determined to extract every joyous bit out of the skein but it took me forever to figure out what to do.

I modified the idea from the Middle Ground Scarf and knit the lace end, tucked it away for later, then knit the other lace end and the entire middle of the scarf until I had only about a foot of yarn left. I grafted the pre-knit end onto my ready-knit scarf and danced around the living room, singing Abba songs, eating chocolate, and trying to make the cat admire the meager two inches of silk left on the table. It was a good day.

Grafting is one of the most brilliant things you can learn how to do in knitting. First attempts normally result in a nervous twitch, but reports of its difficulty are exaggerated. Clever knitters will realize that to graft complex stitches (like cables), you don't need to know anything more. Graft your knit stitches together, and when you come to purl ones, take the yarn to the back, turn the work around and bingo! — more knit stitches. Remember, each stitch is a knit and a purl . . . you need to know how to graft only one of them.

Knitting Rules!

Voilà: a scarf that has two matching ends.

GILDING THE LILY
Five Ways to Add Interest to a Boring Scarf You Already Knit

Boring Scarf Solution 1

Fringe. The jury is out on whether fringe is cool, but I like it and so do cowboys. To add fringe, cut pieces of yarn twice as long as you would like the fringe to be, fold them in half, and, with a crochet hook, pull the looped ends through an edge stitch, then pull the free ends through and yank on them to make a tight knot. Double points if you tie the fringes into an interesting pattern.

Boring Scarf Solution 2

If you're a knitter who dabbles in crochet (or a crocheter who is dabbling in knitting), take advantage of your position as a multi-crafter and think about adding a few rows of some interesting crochet edging to the bottom of the thing. There's no reason not to combine your skills.

Boring Scarf Solution 3

Knit a bunch of tiny squares, circles, or flowers, make 30 pom-poms — in short, create anything you like and sew them to, or dangle them from, the ends or edges of the scarf.

Boring Scarf Solution 4

Knit a lace edging and sew it onto the ends.

Boring Scarf Solution 5

Visit the notions section of a local sewing store and see what it has. Think about big buttons, a bunch of tiny ones, braids, cords, appliqués, and tassels. Stand there in front of the wall and ask yourself, "Could I sew this to a scarf?" Don't limit your thinking.

> **A scarf that has turned out too big is not a failure. It's a shawl.**

SHAWLS

This is my favorite thing about shawls, among the countless great things about them. Shawls are the mighty chameleon of knitting, and virtually anything you knit could be a shawl if you think about it right and can get the thing over your shoulders. Shawls come in many shapes, sizes, weights, and applications and keeping an open mind will have you knitting one (perhaps by accident). Shawls suffer, sadly and inappropriately, from an association with pioneer grandmothers, and this can cause many a fine young knitter to turn her back on them. If you are that kind of knitter, the kind who hears *shawl* and imagines either an 80-year-old woman in a rocking chair or a peasant woman sweeping a dirt floor, maybe it's not that you don't want to knit a shawl, maybe you just need to call it something else.

It's not a shawl, it's a:

Stole. A stole is usually a rectangular piece of fabric wider than a scarf but just long enough to wrap around your shoulders and fasten fetchingly with a pin or brooch. Using the guidelines for Scarf Recipe #1 will make a stole if you do it with more enthusiasm and a certain flair, as the whole idea of a stole embodies elegance.

10 REASONS

Ten Reasons to Knit Shawls

1. Virtually every culture on earth has a history for the shawl. There's the Jewish prayer shawl or *tallis;* a Spanish lace mantilla or *abrigo;* a Gaelic tonnag; and, going back as far as ancient Egypt, the sacred *iraoros* shawl. There must be a reason for this, and you should knit one while we figure it out.

2. It's extremely difficult to pretend to be Mata Hari without one.

3. Shawls can be knit from virtually any yarn you can get and will still look appropriate. I have an Aran-weight cabled wrap, a cobweb-lace triangle, and a copper and gold stole that I imagine myself visiting casinos in. (I don't go to casinos, but the point is that if I were to, this is the right yarn to go in.)

4. There is no more elegant way to cover your shoulders as you and a handsome companion stroll through the moonlit park chatting after the ballet. (Well, yes, I do have a rich fantasy life. Why do you ask?)

5. Even if you don't wear one for leaving the house, you can drape one over the back of a chair to pull over your shoulders on a drafty winter afternoon

Knitting Rules!

without anybody thinking you're a slob who doesn't put away her clothes. (Which is totally what people say when you leave your sweater on the couch.)

6 I can toss a big woolen one about myself as I head to the grocery store and get a *Wuthering Heights/ Cathy-on-the-moors* feel going, instead of my usual "I-forgot-to-buy-cat-food feeling."

7 As with scarves, gauge is almost irrelevant. A shawl that comes out too small is a scarf (or, in the event of a too small circular shawl, a doily) and a scarf that comes out too big can be an afghan.

8 There is no greater welcome for a new baby than a shawl as delicate as it is. I love the look of a tiny wee face wrapped in exquisite lace stitches. Even the simplest of shawls looks better around a baby, and I labor under the delusion that she will keep this shawl all her life, perhaps wear it on her wedding day, or, if it's a boy baby, give it to his bride. I even imagine that I've created an heirloom that will someday hold this baby's baby. It's hard to think of anything more worthy of baby puke.

9 A shawl has no armholes, heels, sleeves, or seams.

10 The most complex and beautiful lace in the world is Shetland or Orenburg, and knitting a shawl in either tradition will change your idea of what you're capable of on this earth.

Pelerine. Technically speaking, a pelerine is a woman's short cape with points in the front. From a knitter's point of view, it's interpreted as a triangular shawl worn draped so the points are at the front. It doesn't matter much, though; you and a few scholars are the only ones who are going to know the word.

Mantilla. This is the word for a Spanish lace shawl traditionally worn over the head and shoulders.

Wrap. The word *wrap* suggests a certain length and coziness. The only shawl I own that I think qualifies as a wrap is of heavy wool and would stand me in good stead in a blizzard. A wrap is a good way to justify an avoidance of lace-weight yarns.

Serape. This is a Mexican shawl, with large bright stripes, worn by men. If your shawl is rectangular and striped, maybe it's a serape. (I love the word so much that even though I'm a middle-aged, five-foot-tall woman and the last person alive who should be wearing a serape, I want one to distraction.)

RECTANGLE

I'm not going to tell you how to knit a rectangle. Do the thinking from Scarf Rescue Hat Recipe #1 (see page 107). Just make it wide enough to cover you from at least neck to elbow and long enough for amusement.

CIRCLE

Knitting a circle without a pattern is — there's no way to get around it — a mathematical concept. Throughout this

All of the ideas for knitting a circular shawl are based on π, but you do not need to know that π is 3.14 (with an infinite, non-repeating decimal), or that π is a common factor in every circular construction. I want you to know that these ideas are based on π, but you don't need to know anything at all about π unless you want to bore house guests into leaving early or triumph at Trivial Pursuit.

book, I've attempted to devise simple ways to dispense with the worst of knitting math and now, in the circular shawl section, I find myself having to face the music. It's as inevitable as the sunrise. I promise to be gentle.

There are three reasonably painless ways to make a circular shawl that lies flat, and all of them are apparently based on the concept of π. (I'll take a moment now to tell you that there are ways other than these three. Because I didn't find them painless, I can't in good conscience pass them on to other knitters. The madness stops here.) That little symbol means *pi* and π is related to circles in that if you divide a circle's circumference by its diameter, the number you get will always be an expression of this ratio: 3.14. I know this because I've been told it's so, but I've never been able to grasp the concept. I tried to understand, but got a nosebleed, which I took as a sign that my brain was trying to escape, so I gave up. Elizabeth Zimmermann, knitting genius and the author of *The Knitter's Almanac*, explained this better than I ever could, and designed a pi shawl that makes perfect sense of the principle, so if you are intrigued, go look there.

If you want your shawl to stay on, no matter what shape it is, knit it so that it's at least the length of your wingspan — fingertip to fingertip with your arms outstretched. This measurement will also be the same as your height.

In virtually all humans, wingspan equals height,

so you don't have to go around measuring people for shawls with their arms poised as if for flight. Simply ask them how tall they are.

Practical experiments and long conversations with delightfully geeky (and patient) friends have taught me the following (if we understand that by "taught" I mean that they told me and I wrote it in the book): Every time the radius of a circle (a line drawn from the center to the outside edge) doubles, the circumference (the distance around the circle) doubles. This piece of information is way more useful than it sounds, even if you aren't a geek.

Circular Shawl: Method 1

What the pi rule means is that if you want to knit a circle, you need to double the number of stitches in a round every time you double the number of rounds you have worked. Practically speaking, this means you double your stitches on rounds 2, 4, 8, 16, 32, 64, and so on. . . . Get it?

Ingredients
You'll need double-pointed needles and circular needles, short ones for short rounds, long ones for long rounds.

How to Do It
Round 1: Start with 4 stitches on double-pointed needles.
Round 2: Since 2 is double the number 1, you double the stitches for a total of 8, using any increase method you like.

There are two easy ways to double your stitches in a round. You can either knit into the front and back of each stitch, which makes a solid round, or you can knit one, yarn over, knit one, yarn over all the way around the round. The second method makes a circle of lacy holes where you increase.

Round 3: Work around with no increase.

Round 4: The number 4 is double the number 2 (the last time you doubled your stitches), so double them again for a total of 16 stitches.

Rounds 5, 6, and 7: Work with no increase.

Round 8: The number 8 is double the number 4, so double your stitches to 32.

There is no law, mathematical or otherwise, that says all the increases must be done on the doubling rows. The rule (as interpreted by a knitter who did a swatch) is actually that you need to have doubled by the time the radius doubles, and this means you can get your extra stitches in anytime you want to, as long as by the time you've doubled your rows, you've doubled your stitches.

From here, you'll nod off and knit around plain or get fancy and do lace or whatever turns your crank, amusing yourself on those plain rows, knitting around and waiting for the next "doubling" rows — 16, 32, 64, 128, and so on —until the diameter of the shawl (from one edge to the other) measures at least the height or wingspan of the recipient, and then call it quits.

Circular Shawl: Method 2

I really don't understand the math behind this one, and in fact I was forced to beg the geeks to stop trying to explain it to me. They kept going and going and it was when I slid from my chair onto the floor and sobbed knitterly sobs that I realized it was okay not to get it. I don't fully understand gravity and I'm still not flying off into space, and I don't get why so many people think Tom Cruise is attractive, but that doesn't change the throngs of people swooning at him. Just because you don't get it doesn't mean it isn't true, and as a result of my failure that evening, you're going to have to live with not knowing why this works. Just trust the geeks — they know.

How to Do It

Cast on (you're going to love this) as many stitches as you want. The number should have some relation to what you'd like the finished radius to be (the line from the center of the shawl to the outside edge), but there's no magic number.

A circle can also be made up of a series of wedges. Imagine a round pizza, cut into slices. Now see each slice as being a wedge of the total shawl. This kind of shawl is worked by making pointed knitted wedges and joining them to form a circle.

The brilliance of this approach is that you may stop and make a semicircle, an almost circle, anything you want, simply by stopping at a desired point. The downside of knitting only a semicircle is that your knitting friends are totally going to figure you bailed out on a circle shawl because you couldn't take the heat.

Row 1: Knit across the row until you get to the last stitch. *Leave the last stitch unknit,* then turn the work.

Row 2 and all even rows: Knit across.

Row 3: Knit to the last **2** stitches, then turn the work (leaving the last two stitches unknit).

Row 5: Knit to the last **3** stitches; turn.

Row 7: Knit to the last **4** stitches; turn.

See what's happening? Each time, you stop one more stitch short of the end. Keep going until you're fresh out of stitches, then knit all the way down the row, across all of your stitches, turn, and knit back . . . and smile at your knitting, because you've made a wedge. Now, poised at the outside edge (where you began row 1), do it again — the second wedge will grow off the first.

Lay down the knitting on the floor periodically as you knit and have a look at it. When you have enough wedges to complete a circle (probably eight, but it could vary and you shouldn't worry about it), **cast off.** Sew the beginning edge to the ending edge and that's it — you've got a circle.

Circular Shawl: Method 3

This method is a bit of a cheat, which should be an indication that I thought it up myself and it might not have much to do with π. I offer it here because it has no math — none, and I thought you might find this a relief. I was thinking about when you decrease for the top of a hat, and if you decrease at the right rate and slope, the top of the hat is a perfect flat circle with a definite pillbox feel. I monkeyed around a little, not with a calculator but with some needles and yarn, and discovered that this works.

How to Do It

Cast on 5 stitches using any yarn and needles you like; gauge is irrelevant. Consider only what you like and nothing more.

For an almost perfect circular start, cast on the beginning number of stitches, join in a round, and work with double-pointed needles until you have enough stitches to go onto a circular. When the shawl is finished, go back to the beginning piece of yarn in the center and, before you weave in the end, thread it through the first round of stitches, pull tight like a purse string, and fasten off. It makes a nice tight start with no hole.

Round 1: Increase in every stitch (for a total of 10 stitches).
Round 2 and all even rounds: Knit plain.
Round 3: *K1, increase; repeat from * around.
Round 5: *K2, increase; repeat from * around.
Round 7: *K3, increase; repeat from * around.
On each subsequent increase round, add one more stitch to the number you work before the increase.

Continue in this manner until the shawl is big enough (or the tic in your eye won't go away). This method is a cheat because, technically, since the work is done in 10 sections it's a decagon (a 10-sided object) and not really a circle.

Because it's the easiest way to solve the problem without math, I simply block it until it looks perfectly circular (which isn't difficult) and make a mental note never to tell a mathematician or an 11-year-old doing a unit on geometry that it's round. They will call you on it.

> If you want a lacy look (without actually doing any lace), consider knitting the yarn on much bigger needles. Naturally, you're forbidden to refer to it as "lace" in knitting circles, but you may certainly lie to non-knitters all you want.

TRIANGLE

There are two ways to go about a triangular shawl, basically speaking. Either you start with your maximum number of stitches and decrease or you start with a stitch or two and increase.

I adore a shawl that gets smaller with each row. It's very good for the morale, but the downside is that you'd better be sure that you have enough yarn or there isn't going to be a triangle, as the shape is forming as you go. (*Note to self:* Find out technical term for shape created when you don't knit the tip of a triangle. Could be an idea if it had the right name.) When a shawl is knit in the increasing manner, if you run out of yarn, you can cast off; the triangle shape is present (if tiny) from the beginning. With a shawl knit in the decreasing manner, all you can do if you run out of yarn is go for the chocolate.

Decreasing Triangular Shawl

To knit a triangular shawl of ever-decreasing size:

Cast on the total number of stitches you think there should be along the long top edge (number of stitches per inch × wingspan in inches).

Decrease one stitch at the end of every other row until you have nothing left.

Increasing Triangular Shawl

Begin with a few stitches, gradually making your shawl bigger and bigger until the thing is as big as your wing-span (or you run out of yarn). The great advantage to this one is that your basic shape remains the same throughout the knitting process, and this means you can call it quits when you run out of yarn (or patience) and no matter where you are, you'll have a triangle.

If you're playing a complex game of derring-do with yardage, this method is sure to get you a shawl. Might be a rather small shawl, perhaps a "shoulderette," but it'll still be a shawl.

There are two ways to knit an increasing triangle. Either start with a single stitch and create a triangle by working an increase one stitch at the beginning and end of every other row or try the following. This method is a more complicated to follow the first time . . .

How to Do It

Cast on 3 stitches for the back of the neck and mark the center stitch.

Work every alternate row plain.

Work the increases on the right side rows like so: Increase one in the first stitch ("yarn over" makes a pretty hole), knit to the center, increase one before and one after the center stitch, knit to the last stitch, and increase one.

This makes a shawl with a center line of increases that will look familiar to you and is the basis for many traditional shawls. It also means (and don't forget this) that each row of the shawl is longer than the one previous, progress seems slower, and those last few rows can go on longer than a kindergarten recorder concert (with about the same emotional effect).

Three Square Shawl Methods

Following are three ways to knit a square shawl.

1 Cast on however many stitches you want, knit until the piece is square, cast off. (I can't believe I typed that.)

2 Cast on one stitch. Knit back and forth, increasing one stitch at the beginning of every row until you have a triangle that's half the size of the square you wanted, then begin decreasing one stitch at the beginning of every row until you have nothing left. Done.

3 You're just waiting for the geeky answer, aren't you? Fine. Cast on 4 stitches and designate each of them an official "corner." You can even give them honorary stitch markers or something. Now knit, increasing one stitch before and after each "corner" stitch on every other row until your square is as big as you want it to be.

A FINAL WORD ON SHAWLS

Recently I was with a whack of knitters and was asked by someone what I would knit if I could only knit one more thing before I had to quit forever. I answered in a heartbeat. (Well, I answered in a heartbeat once the dizziness and nausea from contemplating a life without knitting passed.) I'd knit a wedding-ring shawl. One of the gossamer, cobwebby, lace beauties knit so fine that the entire shawl, the whole thing, millions of stitches and thousands of yards of yarn, can be drawn through a golden wedding ring. They leave me breathless, and in my mind they are knitting's holy grail.

My reasoning was simple. It would take forever to knit, and if I only get to knit one more thing in this lifetime, I'm sure not going to do a hat — it would be over too quickly. I'd have the shawl forever when it was finished, as I couldn't outgrow it, nor would it pass out of fashion. Additionally, there's no such thing as a wedding-ring shawl too big, so I could drag it out as long as I wanted to.

To ice the cake, I'd get to enjoy the magic of blocking a shawl one last time, and enjoy the magic way the pile of ratty-looking yarn, reminiscent of barely wrangled noodles, is transformed by a dunk in water and the process of stretching and pinning it out. The moment a shawl is blocked is still a remarkable one for me, even though I've done it a bunch of times. I think that to go out of knitting on such a magnificently transformative high would be the knitter's equivalent of the way Vikings used to say farewell to a warrior: by sending a burning barge carrying his earthly body off into the sea. I realize that this may be a symptom of a deep obsession with shawls, and I'm okay with that.

eight

SWEATERS

EVERY SWEATER STARTS THE SAME WAY. I go up and down the aisles in the yarn shop (I'm far too attached to my stash yarn to use it for sweaters), pulling out skeins and giving them a squeeze (perhaps a sniff), reading the labels, sighing, putting them back, and continuing to wander down the wall of yarn. Then I find a yarn I really like, realize it comes only in petal pink and violent puce, and put that one back. A couple of aisles down I actually find the right color, but it's the wrong weight of yarn. (I'd rather not discuss what I'm doing in the double-knitting section when I've come here to buy a worsted weight. I think it's the wool fumes.)

Knowing that I have the wrong yarn entirely should lead to immediate rejection, but instead I spend more than a few minutes consulting my pattern and doing a little mental math (if you can believe that) before I realize I could actually convert the pattern to use this yarn, but that I'm going to drive myself batty doing it (and it hasn't been too long since the squinty eye I developed last time went away). So, I stuff that yarn back on the shelf too. This common knitterly ritual — and it has to be common, because there are 14 other knitters in the shop, all sighing and patting and sniffing — goes on for a good long time, and it should. I'm contemplating the beginning of a sweater and that takes a lot of thought. You can throw away a couple of hours on a bad hat that was a mistake from its impulsive start, but a whole bad sweater takes some ingenuity to excuse.

A BIG DECISION

I love this about sweaters. I love that they're a big decision. Sweaters aren't like whipping off a pair of mittens

10 REASONS

Ten Reasons to Knit a Sweater

1. **It's a commitment.** Socks and hats are fun and, in their elevated forms, can certainly be artful, but sweaters are like a marriage (or at least an engagement).

2. **It's an upgrade from an accessory,** and a really good sweater can become like a good friend.

3. **Once you get the hang of it,** knitting your own sweaters makes it possible for you to have garments that actually fit, and sleeves the actual length of your arms. Realizing this was a big deal for me, considering I usually have an urge to phone commercial sweater producers and ask them if monkeys are their sizing models.

4. **You could spend a lifetime exploring all the variations** on sweaters: raglan in pieces, raglan in the round, top-down seamless, bottom-up seamless, cardigan, steeked Norwegian, fine wool English jumpers, Irish Arans, the weird thing you invented when you thought you were doing a cap sleeve but got two pages of the pattern stuck together.

5. **There's a style for everyone.** There isn't anybody who doesn't look good in a sweater. Admittedly, finding the right sweater can be a bit of a process, but at least you get to knit the experiments.

6. When a sweater goes wrong, it's much more spectacular than a wayward scarf. You can laugh about a hat that came out weird for maybe 10 minutes, but an unexpectedly "unique" sweater never stops being funny (once you work through the period of grief and shock).

7. A sweater's a big canvas. If you get an urge to knit an intarsia hockey player onto something you want to wear, a sweater is just about the only thing that's going to work. (Don't laugh. I'm a Canadian. When I was a kid, everybody I knew had a hockey player sweater. Well, except for Renee. She was lucky. Hers had a ballerina.)

8. A baby sweater done in chunky yarn is the fastest high a knitter can achieve.

9. A sweater project offers variety: the challenge of picking up stitches and working the decreases, the almost meditative calm of the plain bits for the body and sleeves, and that familiar urge to strangle yourself with a circular needle when you realize you missed the instruction "at the same time" and the sleeve is 10 inches too long. Good times.

10. A sweater affords the scientific-minded a chance to experience the phenomenon of the Knitting Black Hole. At some point in your work (although you have definitely knit 34 rows since you first noticed), you stop making progress. You knit and knit but the sweater doesn't get bigger. Then, mysteriously, you are released and discover that, even though you've been obsessively measuring every two rows, it's suddenly five inches too long. If you figure this out, let me know. It makes me nuts.

or a whack of socks. Other knitting can be forgiven for flaws: a hat with a weird top is eccentric, a pair of baggy mittens is still functional. A shawl with bad gauge still drapes. Sweaters, though, are really hanging it on the line. A sweater with a bad gauge, a weird neckline, and a baggy front has no charm. It's just bad clothes, and herein lies the rub, the reason that so many people — including me, from time to time — are scared off by sweaters from the word go. Sweaters are clothes, not just knitting, and because there is more to them, there's more that can go wrong. A bad scarf can still be charming on some level and the consequences will never make your breasts look saggy, but a bad sweater has impact.

Don't expect too much of your first sweater. As a general rule, they get better, and each one can exist simply to teach you something. (Goodness knows they aren't always wearable.) Sometimes it's a lesson in gauge, sometimes it's about sizing, sometimes it's the meaningful lesson that only 12-pound supermodels look good in chunky-weight horizontal stripes, no matter how great the colors look together.

A LABOR-OF-LOVE TALE

My first sweater was a nightmare. I had a boyfriend and we had been dating (actually, going steady, which at the time seemed a very important distinction) for about six months. Teen relationships, I realize now, are counted in dog years, with more time passing for the teens than for everybody else. Therefore, a month is like a year and we had been

The Sweater Curse holds that if you knit a romantic partner a sweater before there's a commitment with some sort of legal binding, he will, within days or weeks of your delivering a sweater into a previously happy relationship, dump you and take the sweater with him. As you can imagine, this is quite painful. There really are other fish in the dating sea and people survive painful break-ups all the time. The real tragedy is that he gets away with a great sweater.

going out for six months — we had celebrated our half-anniversary. (Now that I've been married for so long it seems stupid to celebrate a mere half year, but at the time it was hopelessly romantic.) So, I felt our relationship was solid enough that it was time to knit him a sweater.

I went through my stack of books, magazines, and leaflets, in search of the perfect thing. This phase can't be rushed. Sweaters need to be imagined, dreamed over. I'm forever taking hours with this part because I actually know what sweater I want. I can see it in my mind; it's just a matter of finding the pattern that I'm imagining. (I can't tell you how difficult it is to find a designer who's thinking just the way I am.) When I had the right plan, I trotted off to the yarn store for the yarn that the pattern suggested. (I told you I was young.) I found it, and after realizing that it was not only priced out of reach of my discount-store-cashier paycheck, I picked another yarn. The pattern called for 16 balls, so that's how many I bought.

When I got home, I enthusiastically pulled out the pattern and the yarn, piled the balls up around me and gleefully cast on, imagining not just the wonder of the sweater, but also the wonder of how much my boyfriend would love me when I gave it to him. Knitting a sweater takes time and for my more-than-six-foot-tall boyfriend, that time was going to be significant.

As I toiled away, I thought only lovely thoughts. How handsome he would look. How grateful he would be. How he would keep it close to him forever and when we were old he would sit on the porch swing and wear the sweater and our grandchildren would sit beside him in the evening light (they would be visiting us to catch fireflies in the garden) and lean against him (still ruggedly hand-some, even in his old age) and would say "Grampa, tell us the sweater story." And he would. He would tell them it was when I knit him that sweater that he knew I was the love of his life. That I had knit him hundreds of sweaters since, and even a couple of vests, but it was this one, this first one that he loved most, since as he had unwrapped it and seen its soft blue stitches, as he ran his fingers over the wool, he had realized it wasn't just a sweater; it was the beginning of the rest of his wonderful life.

That's what I thought while I knit it. The sweater was going to have a life of love and glory . . . except it seemed just a smidge big. Truth be told, I had purchased chunky-weight yarn when the pattern called for wor-sted, and was too inex-perienced to know the peril my mortal soul was in. To com-pound the problem, my youthful idea of gauge consisted of using the needles called for in the pattern without regard for the type of yarn.

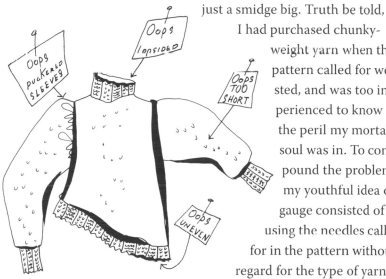

This was very wrong (and resulted in me knitting not just an enormous sweater, but also one so stiff that the pieces wouldn't fold), but I was blinded by love. Plus, he was a big guy. What was the trouble with having a sweater that ended up a little big? It would be comfortable and cozy, like a big hug. (Looking back, I hardly recognize myself.)

Then there was the problem with the neck. It was a little crooked. (It was a little crooked exactly the way that the Godfather was a bit of a criminal.) I thought about going back, but it had been really hard to do the first time and I thought it probably wouldn't matter once I got the neck stitches picked up. *Note to self:* If, when you go to pick up the stitches, if you get the 24 the pattern suggests on one side and a scant 13 on the other, this is a good indication that the neck isn't going to "block out" (the other solution I had in the back of my mind, which too was dreadfully wrong).

I plugged on though, even when one side of a sleeve sort of puckered in a strange way. I tugged at that quite a lot, but I was sure no one would be able to see it if he kept his arms at his sides. I tried to pucker the other sleeve so it would at least match, but it gaped at me without remorse. The other problem (not that it was exactly a problem, because what can stand in the way of true love?) was that I had needed to go back to the yarn shop twice for more yarn (why on earth the fact that the sweater was taking triple the amount of yarn the pattern called for wasn't a tip-off that it was going to be triple the correct size is a question I still can't answer) and that the sweater had now cost me more than three months of part-time income at a crappy job. What we do for love.

When it was done, I was really proud. Too proud, now that I think about how it actually looked. When I tried it on, the arms dragged on the floor (one of them less so than the other; the puckering subtracted some length), and the hem reached almost to the ground. I took it off by letting it fall down and then stepping out of the left side of the badly unbalanced neckline. Still, I told myself, he was a big guy (Jabba the Hut would have drowned in that sweater) and it was the '80s. Oversize was in.

I folded it up, wrapped it in tissue paper, and presented it to my boyfriend with all the pomp and circumstance I could muster. I'll never forget the look on his face. At the time, I was sure it was awe. I'm still sure it was awe, actually. He took in the whole thing, declined to try it on, and three days later dumped me without so much as a nod in my general direction. I still feel bad about it. That was a lot of wool to kiss good-bye.

If you were ever dumped after knitting a guy a sweater, consider the possibility that (Sweater Curse notwithstanding) the problem was with the sweater, not you. The recipient probably took one look at the thing, imagined a lifetime of having to pretend to like (and wear) this sweater and others of its ilk, and saw no choice but to flee into the night.

INCREMENTALISM

When I'm intimidated by the idea of a sweater, I use the concept of incrementalism to overcome whatever is flipping me out. I break down the thing and look at it only in parts. Often, once I look at it in pieces — only the individual pieces — I can pull myself together.

I sit down and read the pattern. Inevitably it says something like *Back: Cast on 89 stitches.* Easy. I can cast on. I cast on all the time. Heck, sometimes casting on is the only part of a project I do! I know several ways to cast on and as long as I don't get bogged down trying to choose among them, I'm good to go.

Next? *Work K1, P1 ribbing for 4 inches.* Dude, I can knit and purl. Adeptly and in order. Bring it on.

Change to larger-size needles . . . Okay, this could give me trouble. There was that time that I changed only one of the needles and the gauge of the sweater alternated in rows as I knit with one 4 mm and one 6 mm needle for the rest of the back of the sweater. It would've been a design feature except that I succeeded in switching both needles on the front and they were different sizes. Still, that was a particularly stunning bit of stupidity and I'm not likely to do that twice.

. . . and work in stockinette stitch until work measures 12 inches from cast-on edge. The trickiest part here is finding a tape measure. Still, my husband has 12-inch feet and I can usually find him. I'll measure off his foot.

The pattern will go on (if it doesn't, that's a sign of a really, really bad pattern) and I'll go on reading it and soon I'll realize that it's not so bad, especially one bit at

Every piece of knitting in the world is based on stuff you probably already know how to do. Never dismiss something as too difficult without breaking down the steps. The only skill necessary for a simple sweater is stamina, and if you've knit a garter-stitch scarf, you have that already. (Hint: The liberal ingestion of coffee and chocolate can occasionally stand in for actual stamina, just come off the sugar high before you try the fiddly bits.)

a time. Sleeves are either tubes or vague triangles that you seam up, backs and fronts are based on squares — taken piece by piece, sweaters are easy.

SKILLS NEEDED TO KNIT A SWEATER

- Casting on and off
- Knitting and purling
- Increasing and decreasing
- Sewing up seams (unless your sweater doesn't have any)
- Blocking

There will be some variations on these, but keep an open mind. Picking up stitches is still just knitting them, and increasing evenly across a row may require some thinking (or a calculator) but it's still just increasing. Even the most complicated knitting instruction in the world is (once you recover your equilibrium) just a combination of the skills above.

Emotionally speaking, I find I need a couple of other skills. Some stamina, for example, which is far, far different from patience, and has merits, as does the ability to do things one step at a time without being overwhelmed by the whole. Really, the one skill, knitterly or otherwise, that you can't learn while knitting is blocking. (Well, and sewing, but you can get out of that if you want to.)

EVERYTHING I KNOW ABOUT BLOCKING I LEARNED THE HARD WAY

In theater, *blocking* is when the director lays out all the movements and places for the actors. In knitting, it's much the same thing. You take all your pieces of knitting and lay them out, check the measurements on the pattern,

10
REASONS

"I Could Never Knit a Sweater": Ten Reasons Knitters Give and What I Wish I Could Say to Them

1 *It's too hard for me.* Yeah. You probably aren't smart enough. Just because knitting was child labor until the 1700s and is still done by impoverished people all over the world who have never seen the inside of a classroom is no reason to think you could get on top of this. If you can read, you can knit a sweater.

2 *It's too complicated.* Remember incrementalism. One stitch at a time, it's the same as knitting a scarf. Except for the buttonholes and stuff, of course, but I still think you can do it and it's better to cross that bridge when you have half a front done and are feeling pretty good about your odds.

3 *Sweaters are too big.* Not by stitch count. Lots of pairs of socks have more stitches than a sweater, and don't get me started on those long scarves. Unless all you've ever knit is four little dishcloths (in which case I'll concede the point), you've done this much knitting before. You need a cheerleader. Let me get my pom-poms.

4 *I've tried and the sweater was crap.* That's no reason to quit. I knit tons of crap. Crap all the time. The path to a good sweater is paved with crap. There's a magic number of crappy things you have to knit before you're released from the crap and can get a good sweater. You must work through the crap to get to the light. It's either that or you don't follow directions well. One of the two.

5 *That's a lot of yarn for one project.* I think you should show me your stash before you talk about how much yarn is too much for one project. Think of the yarn storage space you'll regain if you start knitting sweaters.

6 *If I knit the yarn into a sweater, I won't have the yarn anymore.* I know. It can be painful to let go of stash yarn that you've grown fond of. That's why you should buy more to knit the sweater. Nobody wants you to miss yarn that's emotionally important to you.

7 *I don't like sewing up things and sweaters always have sewing up.* Two words. Circular needle. It's like a miracle.

8 *I don't really like sweaters.* Shut your mouth. Sweaters are the highest form of the knitter's art. If you don't like to wear them, it's your duty as a knitter to force them on others.

9 *I live in Hawaii.* Well, okay, fine, but don't you have an aunt in Wisconsin?

10 *I think shawls are better.* Fair enough, but you're not going to let sweaters beat you, are you?

and then pin or smooth them to the suggested dimensions. Then, either steam the pieces in place after you pin them or pin them while they're still damp from a wash. Blocking can be a serious help to a knitter making up a sweater: it evens things out and lines up edges for sewing, that sort of thing. Knitters often think blocking is going to solve way more problems than it can, and I'm no exception. If I hear myself say "Do you think it will block out?" or "I'll fix it in the blocking," it's a heads-up to me that whatever I'm talking about probably can't be solved by blocking.

HINTS FOR SUCCESSFUL BLOCKING

If your blocking plan involves the word *yank* it probably isn't going to work. This approach to blocking often involves things that are too short or too narrow, and is doomed to failure. Blocking is a subtle art.

> Blocking is kind of like dusting and vacuuming. It makes all your stuff look the best it can, but it's still the same old furniture.

If your blocking plan involves big change — really big change like getting an extra 10 inches into a bustline — it's probably not going to work. Blocking will fine-tune fit but it won't give you an extra 10 inches. Knitting is an elastic form, yes, but with limits. This means that if you're able to pull it enough widthwise to get 10 inches in the chest, you will likely lose several inches in the length. This leads to noticing it's now too short and giving it a lengthwise tug, then seeing you lost the width and pulling there only to see it's too short again. (*Tip:* The number of times a knitter repeats this cycle is related to intelligence. Quit early.)

Blocking won't stop stockinette from curling. I'm

Blocking doesn't fix mistakes. It can make stitches more orderly, smooth out work, make Fair Isle lie nicely, and convince work to hang properly, but in the end you can't rely on it to fix errors, only imperfections. This means if my sleeve cap is hideous because I twisted the stitches when I was picking them up, after blocking I'll still have a sleeve cap with twisted stitches, but they will be very nice and smooth and orderly.

sorry; this is just the nature of stockinette and of stitches like it. There's nothing you can do. You're going to pin it out and steam it and stretch it and then when you pick it up it's going to curl. (Blocking again won't work either. I'm ashamed of how I learned that last one.)

Blocking will absolutely fix a neckline that's a little too chokey, a wrist that's a little too tight, and ribbing that clings annoyingly just under your rear end, making you look like an inflated balloon.

Wool blocks like a dream; acrylic, not so much. Acrylic — and I can't stress this enough — will go limp the minute you try to steam it. This limpness is termed "killing acrylic" and it can't be fixed. Never, ever steam (or iron) to block acrylic.

I don't know why this didn't occur to me before a few years ago, but it was a moment of inspiration when it did. If I'm wondering what's going to happen to something in the blocking and I don't want to wait until I've finished, I block it on the needles. Radical, I know, but it works. Just block the thing as is, right on the needles, and see what happens. If things look good, carry on; when you block the finished item, you won't see that part of it was pre-blocked. If it doesn't look good, my deepest sympathies, but at least you didn't knit the whole sleeve before you found out.

EVENTUALLY . . . YOU WILL KNIT CARDIGANS

If you knit sweaters, the odds are you're eventually going to get it into your head to knit a cardigan. I love cardigans better than pullovers: When I get hot or cold in public, it's much easier to get a cardigan off and on without wrecking my hair or pulling my glasses from my face. Considering how inelegant I am most of the time, I appreciate all the help I can get. A cardigan is infinitely more useful, but it's also a little trickier than the noble pullover. The sticking point, and there's always a sticking point, is that you must learn how to add (pardon me while I suppress a shudder) a button band.

Let's establish my bias. I hate button bands with the same passion and fury I felt when a girl named Cindy and two other pigtailed thugs chased me home from the fourth grade almost every day for a month. I hate button bands where you pick up stitches and knit the bands out, perpendicular to the fronts. They always look like I'm investigating free-form knitting until I've frogged it a dozen times.

To avoid this test of skill, I've accepted that the vertical-strip button band is my alternative. Sadly, there's nothing to love about the vertical band either. Simple instructions, though: Cast on 6 (or 7, or 10 stitches, just enough to inspire you to learn to knit backwards to

When picking up the stitches for a button band, pick up two stitches for every three rows. This is supposed to work, is the rule that most knitters understand to be effective, and will likely bite you hard on the hind parts only about 35 percent of the time. No one knows why. If a band is convex (larger than the front), pick up a few less; if it is concave (smaller than the front), pick up a few more.

avoid turning for the 467th time at the end of the annoyingly short row) and knit back and forth, ad infinitum, until the band, slightly stretched, is the correct length. "Slightly stretched" is a particularly maddening description, isn't it? Isn't that subjective? What if you're kind of high-strung? Relaxed? It is my suspicion that the reason they give this vague instruction is that the exact appropriate length of a button band is as much a mystery to cardigan designers as it is to us.

So here's my thought. Why knit button bands? Really, especially for vertical ones, why wouldn't you just include the stitches for the bands when you knit the fronts? I know it's not going to look quite as fabulous as it would the other way (that "slightly stretched" aspect adds a certain "je ne sais quoi"), and that a team of knitting examiners would be appalled, but what's there to stop me from adding the seven stitches for a band to the stitches for a front and keep them in rib while I knit it up? I'll do the front where the buttons go first, then I'll mark the rows I think should have buttonholes on the other side, and I'll knit them in as I go.

If a button band really makes you twitch, think about putting in a zipper instead of buttons. To do this, add a

After much experimentation, I have determined my own system for determining band length. I knit until I feel like I'm going to scream. Then I have a cup of coffee and knit until I feel bitter, burning resentment. Then I measure, have a little cry, and knit until I feel the apathy of the doomed. This is usually the right length.

Right or Left?

Buttonholes traditionally go on the right front for girls and on the left front for boys. Intrigued by this, I did a little research, wondering why on earth sexism would turn up in buttonholes.

It turns out that because girls were dressed by others (often their buttons were in the back), it was easier for the buttonholes to be on the right of the buttoner. Men however, dressed themselves (buttons largely on the front), so their buttonholes went on the left.

I can never remember which way it goes, but I figure that because we dress babies and children, theirs should be on the right, and because most adults dress themselves, I put theirs on the left. It makes me feel like I'm starting a commonsense revolution for buttonholes.

few extra stitches to the fronts of your sweater (if you aren't adding button bands you need something to make up the width). If your button band was 1 inch, add a half inch of stitches on either side. Knit these in something non-rolling (like garter stitch) as you knit the fronts. When you're done and have the sweater sewn up (if you're sewing) and you get to the part where the instructions are to add the button bands, you can laugh like crazy and yell "Suckers!" (that's my favorite part) and sew in a zipper. It's satisfying.

SWEATER KNITTING IS TRUTH

In life, much happiness is gained by traveling the path to self-acceptance. "Know yourself" is a goal touted by inspirational speakers, therapists, and mothers all over the world, and it turns out there's a way that applies to knitters as well.

KNITTER, KNOW THYSELF

The biggest hurdle to sweater knitting, at least knitting sweaters that fit you, is having a clear understanding of what size you are. Most knitters (including me) seem to struggle with this. I don't know if it's low self-esteem, poor body image, or the simply horrible reality that a sweater too small can't be worn but a sweater too big can be . . . but most knitters overshoot wildly, knitting sweaters far too big for them.

When I decide to knit myself a sweater, I measure my bust, see that it's 37 inches, consult the pattern, decide that I don't want to get burned by making something too small and so pass over the 36 and the 38, and make the

The RGR (relative gauge risk) with sweaters is admittedly high. The consequences of having a gauge accident with a sweater are not the same as with a scarf or a hat. If a hat goes belly-up in the gauge pond, I can find someone else to wear it, or rip it out and try again, without feeling too bad. If you aren't careful about gauge with a sweater, the pain is going to be real, vivid, and acute. The pain is so acute, in fact, that many knitters can't face it and will wear the thing anyway. The only way around the RGR of sweaters is to exercise caution and cultivate acceptance. Measure, swatch, measure, and accept. It's not an easy level of trust to get to.

choice to knit the size for a 40-inch bust. (No way that will come out too small. I'll be able to wear it even if there's a little bit of a gauge accident.) When I'm done and the sweater definitely isn't too small (in fact, it is voluminous enough that while wearing it I resemble a ship under sail), I get disappointed, claim my sweaters never work out and put another mental note in the mental box marked *Why I don't knit sweaters, proof number 17.*

The truth is that I've done it to myself by not achieving the acceptance stage. I'm not a fat 37 or a 37 that's bigger than most other 37s; I'm just a 37, and if I could get my head around that, my sweaters would look a lot better on me. You need to accept the reality of the body you've been given and not pretend it's other than it is. That way, you'll have a great-looking sweater that looks great on you.

It's tricky, and I'm sure Freud would have a field day

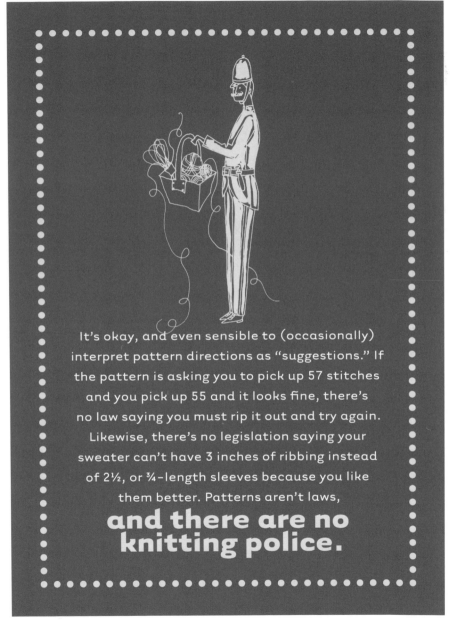

It's okay, and even sensible to (occasionally) interpret pattern directions as "suggestions." If the pattern is asking you to pick up 57 stitches and you pick up 55 and it looks fine, there's no law saying you must rip it out and try again. Likewise, there's no legislation saying your sweater can't have 3 inches of ribbing instead of 2½, or ¾-length sleeves because you like them better. Patterns aren't laws,

and there are no knitting police.

with the closetful of enormous sweaters I've knit. I'm sure the phrase "Napoleon complex" would be bandied about. (How big does this woman think she is?)

If, after some experimenting and adjusting, you find the perfect sweater pattern for you, laminate it. It will serve as the template for many good sweaters to come. I have a laminated pattern that has sleeves the right length, a good amount of ease for me, and a neckline I believe is flattering, and I use it with every sweater I make. I can take the stitch pattern I like from one sweater and plug it into my favorite, and I can compare the width and length of a new pattern to know if it's going to fit the way I like. If I find another pattern I think would be great except for, say, the neck, I use my favorite one in place of it. A good basic sweater pattern that fits you nicely is a tremendous find. Guard it with your life.

THE SPIRIT OF THE LAW

While you knit a sweater is a very good time to come to understand the difference between the letter of the law and the spirit of the law, and knowing that difference can mean a leap for sanity or a crash into defeat.

This concept can be illustrated by the difference between a Saturday night in Toronto and a Saturday night in a small town. Let's say a guy is walking down Queen Street in Toronto. It's a busy street, there's tons of people, it's a hot summer night, and the dude is walking home from the store with a six-pack of beer. Suddenly he gets an idea, reaches into his bag, and cracks himself a cold one. Buddy is walking down Queen Street, drinking a beer, completely sober, hurting nobody. I promise you, if a cop sees that beer open on Queen Street, our friend is going to the Don Jail till Monday morning. The law says no drinking alcohol in public spaces, and that's what the cop is going to enforce. Toronto's a big city. The cop doesn't have time to work out that buddy is sober and harmless. The cop is enforcing the "letter of the law."

Now, switch over to a small town. Same guy, same Saturday night, same beer. Dude's walking down the street, drinking a beer in public, breaking the law. Luckily, this is the only crime being committed in this small town tonight and when the cop sees him, he has time to figure out what's going on. He talks to the guy for a bit and finds out that he's sober and harmless. Because the no-drinking-in-public law is really on the books to keep harmful drunks off the street, and this guy isn't a harmful drunk, the cop reminds our friend that he shouldn't be drinking on the street and suggests he pour out the beer and get along home before he opens another. This is the spirit of the law in action.

How does this apply to sweater knitting? Let's say all the pieces of my sweater are knit and now all it needs is a neck band and button bands. Excellent. I glance at my pattern book and see that the sweater does indeed have a neck band, that it's knit in 1×1 rib, and that you pick up and knit some stitches after joining both shoulder seams. There's some other information there, like how many to pick up, what side the designer thinks I should pick them up from, and how many rows of 1×1 rib she thinks the neck band should have. Those instructions represent the letter of the law. The spirit of the law is basically saying that I should end up with a neck band done in 1×1 rib, not that I should sit here for 17 hours tinking and picking up stitches along the neckline to get the exact number in the pattern, making myself crazy until I'm mean to my husband and hate the stupid little (big) sweater.

It's not that I don't have respect for patterns (well, I have less than most knitters, but then I don't mind ripping out stuff when it looks bad). I understand the law. I understand that someone went to a lot of trouble to work it out for me, and darn it, I appreciate it. Considering, though, that I'm familiar with the law and what it's intended to do, I don't believe anyone meant me to throw my common sense out the window and give myself new wrinkles trying to do things exactly as I'm told, or to disregard the experience I have gained from knitting neck bands in the past, or to have the kind of neck band I'd like. Therefore, I'll pick up as many stitches as seems

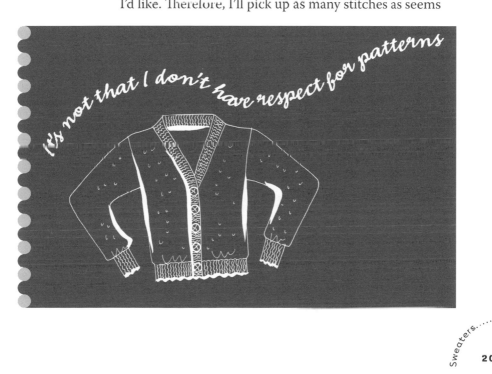

It's not that I don't have respect for patterns

right, and if it looks okay, I'm just going to follow the rest of the instructions that specified a 1×1 rib for, well, as far as I want to.

There are many truisms about sweater knitting, like that the sleeve you've knit and the armhole you've knit should bear a certain relationship to each other, and it would be smashing if I could rip off a list for you to use. The ultimate truth about knitting is that sometimes the finer points of the craft become about "feel." If something doesn't feel right, do it over. If a mistake is bugging you, rip it back or it will always bug you. If, by accident, you find a new way to do something that doesn't match what the pattern is telling you, carry on. You could be inspired. Never be afraid to trust your instincts. Therein lies the path to greatness, and in the end . . . it's only knitting.

I've said it before and I'll say it again.
I hate hearing knitters say they're afraid to try
things in knitting. I know this is a remarkable
statement for someone who lives an entire life
based on the sport, but hear this:

It's only knitting.

One of the beautiful things about it is that (as
long as you don't leave needles lying around)

it's not dangerous.

Leap on! Be afraid of bears, of bungee-
jumping, of faulty wiring in old houses, but
never, ever be afraid of trying something in
knitting. Wool is reusable, your mistakes are
your own, they can all be fixed, and nobody
dies or is fired when you make them. It's only
knitting, and it's one of the few times in your
life when there are no bad consequences
to a mistake.

THE BLACK SHEEP

A KNITTERS GLOSSARY

blocking. The gentle art of setting (by steam, moisture, or mind control) one's knitting and smoothing imperfections. Generally regarded as far more powerful than it actually is, the translation for *I think it will sort out in the blocking* is "I know I'm in trouble but I don't know what else to do."

DPN (double-pointed needles). The original solution to knitting in a circle without a circular needle. They come in sets of either four or five, and are quickly and rudely reduced to sets of two or three. Whichever is more useless.

ease. The difference between your actual measurements and the finished measurements of the stuff you knit. The normal amount of ease for knitted garments is between a minus (for something very tight) and 6 inches (for roomy) — not 22 inches, no matter how much you'd like to avoid a gauge swatch.

entrelac. A technique that involves knitting little squares that run off at angles perpendicular to one another. In its most advanced applications, it can be used as an intelligence test. Anyone who can knit a pair of socks using this technique without resorting to curse words, stomping, or flailing about should (in this knitter's humble opinion) be immediately sent to the United Nations, where her gift may serve the world.

Fair Isle. Technically speaking, a style of stranded multicolor knitting constructed of traditional patterns and "peeries" (small motifs) native to the Fair Isle region of Scotland. Unlike other color work in knitting, all the colors are carried across the wrong side of the work when not in use. Traditionally, this is accomplished in Shetland wool, in the round, and with two colors to a row, and produces intricate and beautiful sweaters, mittens, socks, and hats. Nontraditionally, it's done in any yarn you can get, in any pattern you can imagine, and produces knitters who curse in public.

felting (or fulling). Shrinking wool on purpose.

frog (frogging). Pulling the work off the needles and yanking on the working yarn to undo it. So named because you "rip-it, rip-it." This is done when the mistake is huge or far back, or you're very angry.

garter stitch. The beginner's stitch, the simplest stitch, the stitch that's knitting in its purest, most straightforward way. Accomplished by knitting every stitch, back and forth, every time, forever. Garter stitch is, ironically, trickier on circular needles, on which you must purl each alternate round to make it appear that you knit every stitch.

gauge. The tension at which one knits. Gauge measures the number of stitches the knitter is getting per inch and uses that information to set a standard for matching tension among knitters. Also, an art related to voodoo with rituals (swatching), artifacts (tape measures), and chants.

(The counting. Oh, the counting.) Not to be ignored, as the knitting goddess will frown on it, but neither are you to become obsessed and count swatches to the nearest 16th of a stitch.

grafting. *See* Kitchener stitch.

Kitchener stitch or grafting. A clever way of joining two sets of "live" (not cast off) stitches without a seam. You thread a darning needle with matching yarn, then weave the yarn between the sets of stitches to create what looks like another row of stitches holding them together. You hold the two needles containing the live stitches parallel to each other, with wrong sides of the knitting facing and the needle tips pointing the same way. You're going to weave in and out of the stitches in four moves: two stitches on the front needle and then two stitches on the back. The darning needle is inserted like a knitting needle, as if to knit or purl, then used to pull the yarn through. The first move on a needle slips a stitch off after you pass through it, and with the second move it stays put. Here's how:

On the front needle, (as if to) **knit** (slip stitch) **off** (as if to) **purl** (leave stitch) **on**.

On the back needle, (as if to) **purl** (slip stitch) **off** (as if to) **knit** (leave stitch) **on**.

Repeat these motions, alternating front and back, until you've joined all your stitches, then tighten it up and make it pretty. Once you get the rhythm, you can chant the bolded words to yourself. One tip that makes your grafting look better is to begin with the moves that leave stitches on and end with the stitches that take stitches off.

knitted-on cast-on. One of the simpler methods for beginning knitting. This start produces a firm, inelastic edge. It begins with a single slipknot sitting on the needle. Insert the needle, knit the stitch, and, when you get to the part where you would normally drop the first stitch, place the new stitch on the needle next to it. Repeat. Most commonly executed by accident by beginners mid-row, this cast-on is the most common cause of "stitch gain" known to knitter-kind.

long-tail cast-on. A method of casting on whereby a knitter pulls out a "long tail" of yarn, makes a knot and begins to work with the two ends of the yarn — the tail and the ball end gradually working toward the end of the tail. The amount to pull out for the "tail" is hotly debated, but rumored to be about four times the width of the piece of knitting. No matter how much you pull out, one of two things will happen. Either you won't pull out enough of a tail and will run out of yarn to cast on with five infuriating stitches before you've cast on enough, or you'll pull out so much that the leftover end will dangle annoyingly while you work, until in a fit of pique you cut it off and throw it away, only to run out of yarn at the end of the project by exactly that amount.

quiviut. The soft down of the arctic musk ox, impossibly soft, ridiculously warm, and perilously expensive. It is not gathered by shearing the animals, but rather by picking it from the rocks and scrag after it has fallen from them. This is not what I thought at first, when I had the upmost respect for those whose life's work consisted of hunting, holding down, and shaving the mighty and dangerous arctic musk ox.

RGR (relative gauge risk). A term to express the likelihood of a knitting disaster related to a gauge misunderstanding. For example: A knitter making a scarf out of a yarn she knows well has an extremely low RGR, but a knitter making a fitted sweater with a new yarn, without swatching, and "hoping for the best" while knitting on a deadline, has the highest possible RGR, and faces almost certain disaster.

short rows. Rows of knitting that are only partially worked across before the knitter turns around and comes back. This allows a knitter to fine-tune fitting, turn corners, and create a three-dimensional shape. Not necessarily a shape she was intending, but, of course, three-dimensional nonetheless.

socks. Tubular clothing worn on the feet. The hand-knit variety of these items are occasionally found on the feet of knitters and people they know, but are far more likely to be found in their natural habitat, half-knit on needles. Unlike wolves, people, and swans, who all mate for life, hand-knit socks are unique critters with an almost incredible tendency to appear in singles.

stash. The yarn you've squirreled away for a rainy day. Possessing a stash is not only noble and decent, but a source of inspiration as well. Don't allow others to make you feel guilty about your stash, even if it has reached WHACO (see below) proportions. Practice looking unbelievers straight in the eye and asking them how much paint they thought Michelanglo had. By the way, there are several subgroups of stash. Canopy stash, for instance, represents that upper, transient layer that's usually first in and first out; well-aged stash is yarn that has probably taken up permanent residence.

SABLE (Stash Acquisition Beyond Life Expectancy). Yarn you'll never have time to use. Quite common, and isn't nearly as bad as it sounds. After all, you want to have yarn to bequeath to your children, don't you?

steek. A knitter's shortcut, and a terrifying one. Steeking is when a knitter cuts open her knitting to create armholes or fronts where only a tube existed before.

stitch gain. The infuriating tendency of newbie knitting to grow in stitch count and width by surprising frequency. Can be countered by either frogging (see above) the work or (and I plead guilty to this one) knitting two together on a subsequent row. Not pretty, but it gives you the right number of stitches again. (It's also a one-way ticket to Ruffletown, but there are limits to how many times you're going to rip back something.)

stockinette stitch. A tremendously popular stitch with all the flat knit stitches on one side and all of the bumpy purls on the other. If you're knitting back and forth, this is accomplished by knitting all the right-side rows and purling all the wrong-side rows. In circular knitting, you do this by knitting every single stitch, every single time. You know you're doing it right when you have either entered a state of Zen-like bliss, brought on by the meditative quality of the predictable pattern, or your brain begins to leak out of your left ear out of unrelenting boredom. Prolonged exposure to stockinette stitch can also cause an almost irresistible urge to whack a big honking cable right down the middle of a sleeve.

swift. A wooden or metal yarn holder. Usually it clamps to a table and opens much like an umbrella to accommodate different sizes of skeins of yarn. A knitter places the skein on the swift, pulls an end free, and begins to pull, winding off the yarn into a ball as the swift turns. A swift replaces a family member bitter about the job of holding yarn for you.

tink. *Knit* spelled backwards, and the act of painstakingly undoing your work one stitch at a time. Used when the mistake is small and recent or when you're too afraid (for whatever reason) to pull the work off the needles.

UFO (unfinished object). A project that's incomplete, and proud of it. A UFO is seldom found alone, but instead roams the knitter's home in packs. The discovery of one UFO should be regarded as a warning sign that there are many, many more. There are reports of mythic "one-thing-at-a time" knitters but these are only anecdotal. A thorough search usually reveals several objects the knitter abandoned and consequently banished from memory.

WHACO. An acronym for *Wool Housing and Containment Overload.* This will happen to almost all knitters eventually. It's the state reached when a knitter's stash outgrows her particular ability and her resources to contain it. This is usually a chronic condition, but periods of remission may occur when a knitter runs out of money (and is thus forced to knit some stash yarn) or moves to a bigger house.

wool. A "gateway" yarn that has the potential to lead to alpaca, quiviut, and other natural fibers. Prolonged exposure to the loveliness of wool can also drag you straight down the path to felting, and, in the vulnerable, spinning.

yarn. In a knitting context, anything you can knit. Highly addictive and to be approached with extreme caution and an awareness of one's budget. An important note: Yarn is not to be confused with wool. For, while wool is always a yarn, a yarn is not always wool.

yarn diet. An approach to yarn control known to be ineffective in dropping permanent pounds from the stash. It can lead to dangerous wool bingeing and yo-yo dieting, wherein the knitter holds off on purchases, shrinks the stash, then rebounds to old yarn habits, gains back the merino, and adds nine balls of the silk. Not pretty to watch.

INDEX